Up in the Air

Christianity, Atheism & the Global Problems of the 21st Century

Jakub Ferencik

Amazon Publishing

ISBN-13: 9798683713829
ISBN-10: 1477123456

Cover design by: Canva
Library of Congress Control Number: 2018675309
Printed in the United States of America

Dedicated to
Marek Brezina
1997 - 2019

Table of Contents

Preface

No Howling from God

My mornings started earlier than most who were my age in my youth. During school days in high school, I woke up at 4 am to read the Bible and dissect Christian literature. I meditated on Bible verses and passages for hours in those early still mornings and rarely told anyone that I was praying on their behalf to God. I cherished those quiet moments in communion with Him.

In school, I considered it a personal responsibility to testify to others about my walk with God not only with my words but in how I treated others. My faith was not merely that I chose not to swear, or drink alcohol, or participate in what I thought to be ungodly behavior, like cheating on tests and gossiping about others. My commitment was less abstaining from behavior and more about delighting in different behavior, namely communion with God. I was often found with a book and was happily ostracized because of my commitment to Jesus. I never thought I was unique in this. Nor did I feel particularly burdened. As I said, I may have abstained from the mundane pleasures of my peers, but I was a part of something that I cherished so much more.

My commitment was also seen in that I attended every conference, Bible group, and youth meeting made available to me. I played on every worship group, and at the age of 14, when I was baptized, at times even led my congregation in prayer, as was the custom for those who became members of the church. I urged members of our congregation to recommit themselves and live radically as the early church did. I would rarely receive praise apart from a few elders and my pastor. More often than not, many shrugged and said that my zealousness was because of my young age. It was just a stage, they thought.

I was impressed by my pastors, who could recite answers to what I thought were the most profound questions of life on evil, suffering, chastity, and all the other pressing dilemmas 14-year-olds have. I wanted to be like them in both their clarity and certainty. I knew that the only thing separating me from them was the discipline to spend an inordinate amount of time reading in quiet study probing my deepest questions. And so I woke in the morning to my dark room until I became more sure and outspoken about my views concerning my unanswered questions.

I remember regularly meeting with one of the elders from our church, a youth pastor, every Monday and discussing apologetics, the defense of the Christian faith. I was familiar with contemporary apologists and was, once again, fascinated with the certainty they spoke with. I wanted to find justification for what I delighted in. I had problems with my faith, but they were never detrimental.

In the summers, when we were not busy with school, we would host what we called "English Camps," where we would teach kids English through Bible lessons that would, we hoped, make them curious about biblical issues. I remember barely spending any time at home because of my preoccupation with volunteering and witnessing. Missionaries would come from Texas and Virginia. We would translate their Bible lessons, spend weeks with them, caring for the kids, organizing games in the evenings, and translating through the days. At times I was so exhausted that all I could do for lunch is sleep for a quick hour because of the endless stream of activities. But we loved every second of it.

Every day was an opportunity to witness God's exciting Gospel to my peers. I debated my classmates and teachers on numerous occasions in front of the class about God's existence. We hosted events where members of these high schools would discuss Christianity by the dozens. Sometimes I would host lectures on sex addiction, or the inerrancy of Scripture, sparking what I recall being voracious debate.

I remember one of them who was particularly sincere in his conversations with me concerning God, Mark. He tragically passed away six years later in a skiing accident around the time I started writing this book. Someone contacted me, perhaps a pastor, he did not introduce himself, on whether Mark ever had the opportunity to hear the Gospel from me. I revealed to the unidentified man what was later revealed to me that Mark did not accept the Gospel because he was not persuaded by my arguments or anyone else's. "He had a strong intellect," I told the man. "Who knows what choices he would have made later in life." I tried to comfort him because I imagined that he had a eulogy to write that would be heard by Mark's family. I dedicated this book to Mark.

In my youth, we went from camp to camp, festival to festival, discussing God, breathing God, and living the Gospel. I was not afraid to be ostracized or made fun of. I understood that it was my call as a Christian. Finally, when I was 16, I looked at opportunities to study abroad, perhaps where I was raised in Kelowna, British Columbia, Canada. I do not remember what exactly made me want to study overseas. But I did, and it was a beautiful choice.

I arrived in Kelowna on the 27th of August in 2013, on a hot steamy day. I missed my congregation back home in Slovakia from day one upon my arrival to Canada. Little did I realize that this was the beginning of drastic, unencumbered change. I was beginning to slip from God's tender grasp.

I met many fantastic people in my school, Heritage Christian School, but most of all, I was surprised by how the Christian community there lacked the radicalism and commitment to the Word of God that I saw in many Slovakian Christians. I was torn. I was becoming lonely in the midst of a materialistic society. The community in my school was not as friendly as I hoped for. I was an outsider, and everyone was too socially inept to notice. They were young, in the end. But eventually, they became close friends. I likened some of us to C. S. Lewis, J. R. R. Tolkien, and Owen Barfield, members of the Inklings, a literary group of friends who also shared their faith in God in common. We discussed theological issues for hours and hours and had many wonderful conversations. But my time here came to an end after a short year. I was accepted to the University of Portsmouth.

I moved to Portsmouth on the South Coast of England to live with three of my closest friends from Slovakia in September 2014. I was studying Forensic Psychology, attending lectures with 400 people at a time. I was uninterested, however; The large classrooms made it difficult to pay attention. I started thinking that I should be studying theology but was scared to commit to it. In the end, I thought I could do more good if I entrenched myself in the secular world, and published works from within the community rather than outside of it. After a short semester, I dropped out of Portsmouth and worked. I was broke. At the time, I worked at a fish and chips restaurant, a bar, and as a cleaner. I cleaned in a grocery store, bar, and private school, always changing depending on the month and amount of work.

I would often have to clean dreadful filth from the toilets in the bars. But at the time I did not mind it since I did not know a different life. I was young, and I needed to pay rent. While I stayed in Portsmouth from September to April, I could not afford one day off. Every day I went to work. Whether I was sick, whether it was Christmas, whether it was New Years, I went to work. God was my comfort.

On one of those days, I was reading a biography on C. S. Lewis. All my roommates left Portsmouth, going back home to be with their families or on vacation. I was staying in Portsmouth alone for two weeks or so. I read about the Trout Inn in Oxford in this biography, where Lewis, Tolkien, and others would drink beer and discuss their work. The name of the pub was familiar to me. A friend of mine worked there the previous summer. I wondered, maybe if I give them a call, ask if he could give me a reference, that I could get a job there. Sure enough, they were hiring. I hopped on the earliest bus that took 6 hours or so to Oxford for an interview.

I came in for the interview and landed the job. I went back to Portsmouth, packed my bags, traveled back, and moved to the Trout. Some of us lived in the pub, making it a majestic experience.

My first month or so in Oxford was interesting, to say the least. For a timid Christian young boy to move into a community of some 40 young adults working in a restaurant from all over the world was both threatening and exhilarating. For one, my room was covered with large posters of naked women because my roommate fancied it at the time. And that can be shocking to walk into for anyone especially my Christian sheltered eyes.

In those early months, I was an outsider. But I didn't mind it. I worked. Then I read. On days off, I went to the city center in Oxford to explore. One of the earliest days, I stumbled on a local public library and took out a biography on Napoleon and managed to finish reading Tolkien's *Return of the King*. But my primary source of comfort was John Piper. I read the *Romantic Rationalist*, which was on C. S. Lewis, relishing on his ability to use words in a way that showed the beauty of Christ to the world. I cherished those books dearly, sitting in parks in the beautiful Wolvercote. I would take long walks and jogs alongside the Thames River, in Port Meadow, watching the sunset sing in red colors. And God was with me, or so I thought.

It was not once that I walked by the Radcliffe Square to City Church for tea, or the other side of Oxford, passing Magdalen College and the infamous Magdalen Bridge. I sat untouched by the world's troubles sitting in St. Mary's Church just past the city center. I felt joy as I was discovering new places in Oxford. I would sit in the oldest libraries, listen to choirs sing in extravagant churches, and think, how lucky am I to be here.

But throughout this time, I also felt increasingly uneasy about my faith. I felt as if I was a mere child experiencing light for the first time, reborn into a world of dark hostility. My coworkers were vicious to one another on a level that I had never experienced before. There was so much hate. I was being awoken to a reality that many live in and experience every day. I thought of myself as the young protagonist in James Joyce's *Portrait of the Artist as a Young Man*, struggling with my faith, my sexuality, and the lies of my upbringing. I felt a darkness disguised in the beauty of the richness of the stars. The beauty was to be enjoyed but never entirely because of the anxiety of my youth.

Slowly, I started feeling that God became distant. I would pray, and there would be no answer. I thought maybe my faith was gone; I was scared of what my life would come to. I was tempted by what I thought of as worldly pleasures. I loved the taste of Guinness, cigarettes, and all that is associated with the rebellious youth. It was the clubs, the beer, the food, and the traveling that I was becoming increasingly in love with. I worked hard and learned to enjoy the fruits of my labor in new ways. We celebrated ourselves, our accomplishments — or things that seemed like accomplishments.

I started being happy without God. I could not find happiness so much in myself because I did not like myself. I wanted to find my happiness in something that I found outside of myself, in living and admiring the wonderful city of Oxford, in the conversations with close friends, and in the reading of great literature.

I was buying any piece of literature I could on how to create happiness. How do I construct it for myself? I met Walter Hooper, the late secretary to C. S. Lewis, who introduced me to Eric Metaxas, one of my Christian heroes at the time. Hooper was envious of my living spaces at the Trout. "What a romantic place to live at?" he said enthusiastically when I had the wonderful experience of talking with him briefly at the Socrates in the City event in Oxford, October 2015. There were many wonderful moments in Oxford that seem like a distant dream now, a reality that I could only hope for. And my experience there changed me. This was only the beginning of my personal search for joy.

My time in Oxford was a dream, and I have been back many times since. But at the time, I saw that I had no future there. I wasn't enrolled in school and worked at a job that wasn't bringing me fulfillment. I was wasting my efforts. I did not know where to go. It could not be Slovakia, I thought. So, I put my fingers on a place that I missed the most, the wonderful valleys of the Okanagan. But first, I went back home to Slovakia for a month or so.

My brief visit to Slovakia was a time that reflected how little I understood why I abandoned my faith in the first place. I talked to everyone I could about my new ambivalence to faith; I wanted to know whether my thoughts were substantiated. I have always loved conversation, and the people in my home country graciously provided that to me. After my month of conversing over coffee, tea, and beer in Slovakia came to an end, I went back home to those valleys that I so missed.

I came back an unbeliever. On my way to Vancouver, in May 2016, I revisited Christianity through the work of the Christian writer, Charles Colson, in *The Good Life: Seeking Purpose, Meaning, and Truth in Your Life*. This was a very turbulent time for me. I was without a job, dropped out of university, and did not have a clue of what to study. By the end of the summer, I was already identifying as a Christian again.

In August 2016, I reread *Mere Christianity*, by Lewis as I took a trip to visit some friends in the colorful green coastal city of St. John in New Brunswick, Canada. I remember reading Lewis alone among the benches in the church, still pondering whether God was the answer to all my lifelong questions. I had a few conversations there with some pastors about religion and my persuasion because my close friend worked for the church, teaching English to immigrants coming into Canada, among other things. Interestingly enough, I also remember reading Albert Camus' *Myth of Sisyphus* at this time, on the beaches of New Brunswick, with the breeze and sun on my face. Was I Sisyphus? I didn't want to be condemned to a life of misery where simple tasks become dreadful burdens. Was my life meaningful?

When I came back from the East Coast, I was urged to dive deeper into Lewis and read *Surprised by Joy*, his lyrical autobiography about how he became a Christian, quite literally, how he was surprised by joy. I wanted to see whether there was any joy in Christianity for me. For Lewis, Christianity was not a strictly intellectual adventure. Instead, it was a journey to a fulfilling relationship with the Creator himself. Lewis differentiated between temporary happiness and lasting joy, which he thought Christianity was best able to guarantee.

I wanted more, however. I stopped reading apologetics altogether for some time. Instead, I turned to the works of Dostoevsky, Kierkegaard, and Hemingway, among others. I wanted to expand my intellectual horizon and read books I was not naturally inclined to read. Or, in the words Lewis, I wanted to become "a thousand men" by reading widely and seeing what they saw in the world (*An Experiment in Criticism*).

The main book that I credit to opening my eyes to the intellectual depth of atheists was *The Age of Atheists* by Peter Watson that I started reading in November 2016. I worked in a coffee shop at the time and read it frequently when customers failed to enter through our doors. I was surprised by how much there was to secular thought and how far in history its grasp was.

In the end, I don't recall ever managing to make a final decision whether to be a Christian or not. Time made me more sure of my agnosticism toward faith in the Christian God. I have now been studying philosophy and political science for four years. These years have both been challenging and rewarding. They entrenched me in my belief that we should speak slowly and carefully about these issues. Things are often much more complicated than they seem at the outset. Reading more so that you know less and are less vitriolic and adamant about your views is one way to summarize my time at university.

Throughout my life, I have been having long conversations about religion. I discussed these subjects with friends, family, peers, and mentors for as long as I can remember. In all my discussions, I've realized that it's difficult to persuade. In the end, we often agree with conclusions because of reasons we aren't fully aware of. Often, we don't even recall the reasons for believing what we do in the first place. And when we are challenged, we feel as if our identity itself is threatened.

That is why I think we need to be charitable. Many of us do not know. The question for me, is not whether Christianity is true for you. You may know the arguments for your belief, or you may not. The question is whether Christianity has any valid place in the 21st century. Christianity will not go away until it is irrelevant.

Many of the writers that I grew up with have passed away. And each time one of them passes away, it affects me in some way. They all hold a nostalgic place in my heart. Their clarity and delivery assured me that there were answers. Little did I know that others were as certain, if not more, as they were. The American Reformed theologian, R. C. Sproul, whom I cherished growing up, passed away in 2017. I owe many of my theological leanings to this one man and the work he did at *Ligonier Ministries.* The political advisor to Richard Nixon and later founder of the *Prison Fellowship,* Charles Colson, whom I mentioned before, passed away in 2012. I remember reading work by him extensively and being fascinated by his arguments. Two personal heroes of mine, Ravi Zacharias and J. I. Packer, both passed away as I was writing this book. In fact, the first book I remember reading on Christianity was Packer's *Knowing God*; His intellectualism became a staple of Western evangelicalism. I owe some of my curiosity to these intellectuals, and I will cherish their influence despite my differences with their views. With these losses, Christians should hope for new communicators that will be as prolific and effective as these intellectuals. Otherwise, Christianity very well may lose its foothold in the lives of others as it did in my life.

Most importantly, if Christians want to be challenged about their beliefs, they should aim to leave their communities and see if their views are not merely the result of social cohesion. I believe they will be challenged and aim for a more nuanced understanding of this world if they do so. We are not always right, and our social predicaments stifle our ability to see clearly. Let's continuously remind ourselves of the profound truth behind this limitation

Introduction

Change – dramatic, basic, overarching change, is today's ranking fact. Everywhere old moorings are breaking loose, deeply entrenched attitudes are being shaken, traditional patterns of social life are gradually giving way and being replaced by new. Samuel S. Hill, writing in the mid-1960s[1]

The 20th century is what historians call the "long century." Wars permeated societies, genocides became alarmingly commonplace, unprecedented nuclear wars horrified millions, and technology made video footage of these realities accessible worldwide, awakening many to horrors we could have never imagined. The 21st century will challenge us in similar ways and may even impact us to a much more significant degree. Our ideological battles are far from settled despite the relative ease of access to expert scholarship today. We are increasingly divided and polarized across the world. Something is changing in both the political space and spiritual space. We are lonelier than ever before and prone to demonize those with opposing moral biases; We refuse to listen, let alone read the "opposition"; And we jump to conclusions.

In this century, we will have to pay close attention to threats that were once unimaginable, from ubiquitous internet surveillance to artificial intelligence, to automation and the real danger it poses in taking away millions of jobs, to our international institutions not being capable of effectively dealing with the severe problems those who flee war-torn countries face. The list of problems we are facing is endless.

In this book, I am talking about some of what I consider to be the most pressing threats and how Christianity and atheism specifically as ideologies can challenge these threats. Atheism, notably, is not a strict belief system. The only thing that atheism does is reject the existence of gods. I could have been more precise in my analysis by specifically talking about humanists throughout this book. But the problem there would be that many atheists do not describe themselves as humanists, they only disagree with the existence of gods. Hence, I decided to stick with the term atheists throughout this text because it is more expansive.

We have good reason to assume that religion is not going away anytime soon despite the predictions and hopes of many secular thinkers from Bertrand Russell to Richard Dawkins. In this book, however, I am not discussing religion broadly, nor am I talking about Christianity specifically. Rather, I am discussing the influence of the Christian right or Christians that are socially conservative. And my analysis does not extend to a global study; Instead, I look at what I know best, which is the West, specifically, the United States of America. I believe that because of the media focus, influential university institutions, and monetary funds, that the U.S. has a strong Christian right group and that the future of socially conservative views in the West rely primarily on the Christian right in the United States.

Of course, we have some reason to believe that socially conservative views will not prevail merely because of Christianity. Other religions also stress sexual chastity, religious duty, and holiness. For my purposes here, however, I will not consider these other religions nor will I talk about many ideologically divergent denominations within Christianity. Many roman-catholics and eastern-orthodox Christians also hold socially conservative views that I could also consider but the book would end up being too long for a digestible reading. In a world where less and less people are reading, I did not want to fall into the trap of perfectionism. A more academic analysis would have to consult these differences in denominations for a more complete grasp of the predicament between Christianity and the 21st century. That is perhaps for another book.

Our Fundamentals

I have divided this book into three parts. Part A, Our Fundamentals, tackles our reasoning and morality. I start with these two topics and I contrast the Christian right's view and what could be the atheist's view on these two topics. If we cannot figure out our fundamentals, whether there is indeed a way to justify rational thinking and moral behavior, we cannot discuss the topics in the rest of the book.

I should mention that there is no one view of the Christian right, nor is there one view of the atheist, since there is no established dogma or institution that is in charge of atheists. The Christian right largely agrees on many ecclesiastical and doctrinal issues but they also have their own discrepancies. From episcopalians to southern baptists to certain methodists and lutherans, not to mention others, each denomination will prescribe different traditions and scriptural interpretations to followers. But the crux of the message of these protestant denominations is consistent.

Some of these consistent interpretations in dogma are: beliefs in absolute moral truths; that Jesus, the Holy Spirit, and the Father are one (the Trinity); that God is all-knowing and all-powerful; that Jesus was without sin; that Satan exists; that salvation is a gift and cannot be earned; that every Christian has a duty to spread the Gospel; and that the Bible is without error in its teaching. For the most part, evangelical Christians agree on these issues. There are always exceptions, of course.

Our Priorities

In the second section, Our Priorities, I discuss human rights, animal rights, man-made climate change, and nuclear war. I touch on the history of human rights, the development of the legal term, how the term is accepted today, and whether Christians prioritize human rights. I similarly look at some of the history of animal rights, the term 'human exceptionalism' in conjunction, and how factory-farming is linked to man-made climate change. Then I discuss nuclear war, the rationalization for 'just war,' and why we should have a healthy degree of worry over the outbreak of nuclear war in the 21st century.

Our Everything
In the last section, Our Everything, I address the fundamental questions behind the meaning of life and the fear that atheism will necessarily result in depression, loneliness, and moral ambivalence. I look at whether the Christian right, or even Christianity broadly, has any way of giving people true meaning in their lives. I look at various ways we can each strive to achieve personal happiness. Then I compare each of these fields from within the Christian framework and the atheist framework.

Why These Topics?
The topics I chose to write about in this book are urgent but there are many more that need our attention. For example, I briefly mention Putin, Bolsonaro, Orban, and other right-wing populist demagogues in this book but I by no means do the issue justice. Similarly, I could have focused more on the economic superpower, China, and its disturbing suppression of free speech and minority-groups. If you are troubled by what America has done when it was the global superpower, imagine what China will do when it by far surpasses the rest of the world in military strength.

I could have also discussed volcanic eruptions, asteroids, terrorism, cyber-hacking, sex-trafficicking, child-pornography, and other global problems to humanity. In future editions of this book, I would like to include more topics and some of these are at the top of the list.

The Focus on Christendom
Before diving into the book, I also want to settle whether dis-

cussing or focusing on Christianity is important. It wouldn't be if Christianity was going away anytime soon. However, Christianity's disappearance is not clear. In fact, Christians are far from receding from the world, let alone the public square. Christianity has been rapidly growing in Africa and China which have a much higher birth rate than in most Western countries. So, we can assume that Christianity will survive in this century and perhaps even prevail.

In this book, I plan on discussing whether believing in God in the way that the Christian right proposes is the best thing for the future of society. In order to do that, I think that it is important to represent the Christian right's beliefs in the best possible way. For obvious reasons, many will think that the Christian belief that I am representing here is not what they hold to be true. Simply put, there are too many discrepancies within the Christian community, to appease everyone. I could be writing in defense of liberal theology, or conservative theology, roman-catholic, episcopalian, baptist, systematic or reformed theology, or methodist theology, and so on. Every single one of these branches within Christianity differs from one another in different ways. Some accept that Mary should be prayed to, others that infants should be baptized, others that humans do not have free will, or that hell is a metaphor. For the purposes of this book, it would be difficult to answer each and every one of the denominations and the differences they have with one another.

Throughout the book, I often claim "The Christian believes ..." and use the terms 'Christendom' and 'Christianity' interchangeably with the 'Christian right.' I understand that fundamentalism as we know it in America and the rest of the world today is different from Christendom historically. However, the similarities in ideologies and the emphasis of turning to figures such as Luther and Calvin or Spurgeon for the exegesis of texts by the Christian right, leads me to think of them as similar terms. Notably, a more thorough examination of these issues would differentiate further than I did in this volume.

Why I Chose to Write This Book

I am writing this book because I myself wanted to read something like this but could not find anything remotely similar to it. When secular critics discuss religion, or even Christianity specifically, they are rarely balanced. Understandably, they have animosity toward Christianity's, at times, demeaning doctrine. But Christianity has a lot that is commendable and we should be intellectually honest enough to acknowledge as much.

Secondly, I am writing this because of the incredible divisions we have in society. It is truly astounding that we are not willing to listen to one another. I want this quote from John Stuart Mill to guide you in reading the views of the "opposition" throughout this book. While you read this book, remember that we all have more to learn and that we all make cognitive mistakes. It's time that we become more charitable to one another:

> He who knows only his own side of the case knows little of that. His reasons may be good, and no one may have been able to refute them. But if he is equally unable to refute the reasons on the opposite side, if he does not so much as know what they are, he has no ground for preferring either opinion. ... Nor is it enough that he should hear the opinions of adversaries from his own teachers, presented as they state them, and accompanied by what they offer as refutations. He must be able to hear them from persons who actually believe them ... he must know them in their most plausible and persuasive form. (*On Liberty*)

The philosopher Donald Davidson similarly advanced the argument that when arguing with the opposition, we should privilege the interpretation of the argument that makes it seem the most reasonable.[2] The position I take is the same in this book.

David Baggett and Jerry L. Walls perfectly point out that public debates on stage and over social media are often zero-sum games and that we should adjust our relationship to them accordingly. Instead, they write that discourse thrives in the "richly relational context of committed colleagues or friends who treat one another with respect, good faith, and cordiality; who tend to have as much to learn as to teach; who are willing to invest the requisite time; perhaps we even care for one another; who, in some real sense, are rooting for their opponent in a collaborative effort to apprehend the truth."[3]

I hope to have done this throughout the book. I hope that our discourse changes in this century so that we have effective conversations marked by intellectual humility so that we are better able to cohabitate with one another.

I want to end this introduction with a manifesto from *Enlightenment 2.0: Restoring Sanity to Our Politics, Our Economy, and Our Lives* by Joseph Heath. I benefited from this book and wanted to share Heath's careful reasoning and the manifesto he leaves us with at the end of his book. I want that same perspective to shape how readers read this book:

> Our era, which began and has developed under the banner of the Enlightenment, first invented liberal democracy, then took it as its political ideal.

> But we have become enslaved by speed, and have all succumbed to the same insidious virus: Fast Life, which disrupts our habits, impairs our concentration and forces us to consume information in ever-smaller packets.

> To be worthy of the name, we *Homo sapiens* should rid ourselves of speed before it reduces us to a species in danger of extinction.

> A firm defense of quiet, rational deliberation is the only way to oppose the universal folly of Fast Life.

Our defense of reason must rest on three pillars. First, we must better *understand* the conditions that make it possible. Second, we must *deliberate* about how to improve those conditions. And finally, we must engage in *collective action* aimed at bringing about those improvements. Only in this way can we banish the degrading effects of Fast Life.[4]

Part A

Our Fundamentals

Chapter 1

Christianity & an Age of Unreason

[God] catches the wise in their craftiness. 1 Cor 3:19

Where is the one who is wise? Where is the scribe? . . . Has God not made foolish the wisdom of the world? . . . the world did not know God through wisdom, it pleased God through the folly of what we preach to save those who believe. 1 Cor 1:20-21

Imagine a world where we stop inquiring into the wonders of life: how life came to be, how societies developed, how our ancestors survived, or where we received our moral intuitions from. This world would arguably be unlivable or, at least, quite unsatisfactory. We would not have long conversations into the night about exciting questions we disagree on with our close friends. For some reason, we find it satisfying to understand the world we find ourselves in.

Because of the rapid prevalence of social media in society, many social commentators are starting to think that our reasoning capabilities are deteriorating. As Heath's manifesto in my introduction warns, we see an increase in fast thinking and a "Fast Life" regarding social and political issues. It's hard not to. *Twitter*, *Facebook*, and the rest of social media promise conversation when, in reality, most of what they end up manifesting are echo-chambers and shouting matches. Many are losing hope for careful thinking. Leading intellectuals across the political spectrum from Jonathan Haidt, Bobby Duffy, Joseph Heath, Keith Stanovich, Daniel Kahneman, and others, say that strict objectivity is a lost cause. That view is not shared by everyone, however. And Christians are particularly disinclined to stand by the research that suggests it because of their distaste for anything that remotely resembles relativism.

We may find ourselves in a society that stops inquiring into the wonders of life. It is hard to tell for sure. Many writers have warned us of this trend, but we do not know if this is just the all-too-human tendency to think that our young are simply stupider than we were in their age. Al Gore, in his book *The Assault on Reason*, warns of the decline of reason in political discourse, Andrew Keen in *The Cult of the Amateur*, looks at the problems with group thinking and herd mentality, others follow suit.

Susan Jacoby in *The American Age of Unreason*, for example, makes a case for a steady incline in intellectual ambivalence in America. Only 57 percent of adult Americans had read a nonfiction book in the past year, she claims.[1] Belief in man-made climate change had declined from 70 percent to less than 40 percent in the past decade.[2] Jacoby explains that our tendency for conversations is also declining.[3] In fact, the Harvard political scientist Robert Putnam showed that right-wing populism, the dreaded political shift in society, is directly connected to weakening face-to-face interactions that started increasing in the 1960s.[4]

Without conversation, people turn to the only source of information they can muster in today's age: the polarized media. Indeed, the instant gratification of the media is rewarding society more rapidly and with less work than the joys of reasoning about everyday questions concerning life, morality, and our place in this world.

Christian thinkers will love to blame secularization for this impact on society. For myself, that connection is less clear, and the primary reason I am starting this book with whether Christianity can provide a consolable place for reasoning in the world in the 21st century. As a Christian, I cherished reading about God, getting to know His character, and how He wants His followers to live. As I touched on in my essay preceding this book, *No Howling from God*, I found immense comfort in thinking about biblical issues as a teenager. I know that many Christians do not share these natural inclinations. The Bible does speak of God's spiritual gift of teaching for those that have intellectual tendencies, in the end (1 Cor 12:28). Despite this, the Bible calls on all Christians to reason, which, if your knowledge of Christianity primarily comes from popular secular writing, may come as a surprise to you.

Many prominent atheist thinkers have thought that religious faith and reason are fundamentally at odds with one another. Michael Shermer, in his book *The Moral Arc*, writes that Christian reasoning "promoted" and "justified" the Crusades, the Inquisition, witch hunts, and Protestant wars.[5] Richard Dawkins, in *The God Delusion*, writes that religious faith does not depend on rational justification.[6] Dan Barker writes in *Mere Morality* that "Purely religious teachings are most often divisive and dangerous," suggesting that religious teaching is not based on reasonable argument.[7] These passages are in many ways direct attacks against the Christian's identity, relationship with God, and communities. No wonder they are not persuaded. Barker's statement, for example, is correct. Yes, Christianity has often been divisive and dangerous. However, it is not only divisive. But I will touch on that later on in the book. For now, let's turn to whether Christians can stir us away from the supposed age of unreason that is enveloping society.

Christians Are Called to Reason Well

Christians are not merely called to think about everyday issues as the rest of us are free to. Yes, of course, Christians can be world-renowned thinkers on biology, mathematics, or physics. Indeed, many Christian apologists boast prestigious academic careers, whether that is Francis Collins, the director of the Human Genome Project, John C. Lennox, the renowned Christian thinker and Oxford mathematician, Sir Robert Boyd, the Vice-President of the Royal Astronomical Society, or Isaac Newton, the "father of modern science," who wrote more on theology than he did on physics.

However, when it comes to everyday Christians and what the Bible expects of them, it is not purely to think about global concerns. Indeed, it isn't easy to establish the primary area of focus for the Christian. Christians are called to "think" about whatever is honorable, just, lovely, commendable, of excellence, and worthy of praise (Phil 4:8). However, that seems to include just about everything that edifies others. It is clear that along with thinking about earthly matters, such as mathematics, physics, and the rest, which are by no means exclusive to Christianity, Christians are also obligated to think about heavenly things, setting their minds on things that are above (Col 3:1-4) and to a "mind" reminiscent of Jesus Christ, their Lord (Phil 2:5). Thus, the Christian priority is not merely to understand this world since this world will fade away. Nonetheless, they are still called to think. Indeed, there are many passages in the Bible that call for a life of the mind for the Christian:

> Do not be conformed to this world, but be transformed by the renewal of your *mind*, that by testing *you may discern* what is the will of God, what is good and acceptable and perfect. Rom. 12:2

> Try to discern what is pleasing to the Lord. Eph. 5:10

> And it is my prayer that your love may abound more and more, *with knowledge and all discernment*, so that you may approve what is excellent, and so be pure and blameless for the day of Christ, filled with the fruit of righteousness that comes through Jesus Christ, to the glory and praise of God. Phil. 1:9-11

We have not ceased to pray for you, asking that you may be *filled with the knowledge of his will in all spiritual wisdom and understanding,* so as to walk in a manner worthy of the Lord, fully pleasing to him, bearing fruit in every good work and increasing in the knowledge of God. Col. 1:9-10

For this very reason, make every effort to supplement your faith with *virtue, and virtue with knowledge.* 2 Pet. 1:5

I am going to confront you with *evidence* before the LORD. 1 Samuel 12:7

Let us *reason* together. Isaiah 1:18

Love the Lord your God... *with all your mind.* Matthew 22:37

Jesus said: '*believe on the evidence* of the miracles.' John 14:11

Paul '*reasoned... explaining* and *proving.*' Acts 17:2-3

[D]efending and *confirming* the gospel. Philippians 1:7

Stop *thinking like children.* In regard to evil be infants, but *in your thinking be adults.* 1 Corinthians 14:20

[B]e ready to *give answers* to anyone who asks questions. Colossians 4:6

[A]lways be prepared to *give an answer* to everyone who asks you to give the *reason* for the hope that you have...' 1 Peter 3:15[8]

[The Scriptures] able to give instruction in sound doctrine and also to rebuke those who contradict it. Titus 1:9

Christians are repeatedly advised to value reason

throughout Scripture. Many, even the most important Church leaders such as Augustine of Hippo, Thomas Aquinas, John Calvin, Martin Luther, George Whitefield, and Charles Spurgeon, failed to follow these principles consistently. But their mistakes in reasoning are not enough to dismiss the Bible's call to reason well. In the end, along with being influential Christian thinkers, they were men of their time and era.

Thinking, therefore, Knowing God: Knowledge That Saves

So what is the place for thinking in the Christian life? The evangelical preacher and author John Piper writes that "thinking is essential in knowing God."[9] By definition, you cannot know God if you do not think about Him. In a way, then, this dependency is similar to the French philosopher, Rene Descartes', infamous epistemological claim, "I think; therefore, I am." For the Christian that can be reworded as, "I think; therefore, I am able to know God." Thought is necessary for belief. That seems incontrovertible. So it would be a stretch to say that Christians cannot provide a consolable place for reasoning in the 21st century since thinking is necessary for being a Christian in the first place.

However, the Bible is also clear that it is not only a *relevant* source for acquiring knowledge but a *necessary* source. In other words, the Bible suggests that real knowledge only comes from the Bible. That is not to say that knowledge concerning the natural sciences comes from the Bible, but rather that the kind of knowledge that counts does.

The systematic theologian, Wayne Grudem, goes so far to say that "true wisdom" can only be gained through a "personal relationship" with Christ.[10] This is based on some biblical understanding. Paul writes that God is "the only wise God" (Rom. 16:27; Rom. 11:33). The Bible further echoes that "The fear of the LORD is the beginning of wisdom" (Ps. 111:10) and that "the knowledge of the Holy One is insight" (Prov. 9:10) because "[in] Christ . . . are hidden all the treasures of wisdom and knowledge" (Col. 2:2-3). It does not seem like a stretch to say that those who do not follow God's path or *know* Him personally are not capable of *true* knowledge. If God is the only one that is wise and knowledge is only found in Him, this logically follows.

For obvious reasons, the claim that "true" wisdom only comes from God can mean several things. As was mentioned above, we can safely assume that it does not mean that Christians will necessarily be better at algebra or chemistry. This knowledge is referencing the wisdom to be able to know that God is real. So, we can call it "knowledge that saves" for our purposes here. The knowledge in the Bible can also reference moral insight into how you should behave. Indeed, the Bible is full of commandments because this was its original purpose. Along with showing people the wonders of God and His work on Earth, it guided people to behave in unity.

The Wisdom/ Knowledge of the World

Along with the message that the Bible is a necessary source for "knowledge that saves," we must also understand the Bible's relationship to secular knowledge, or knowledge attained without any reference to the Bible.

For the early Christians, pagan wisdom was foreign to the wisdom of God. The early theologian, Tertullian (AD 160-225), asked, "What has Jerusalem to do with Athens?" implying that the philosophy of the Greeks was anathema to that of Christ.[11] Paul describes humankind ("man") as those who "by their unrighteousness suppress the truth" (Rom 1:18). According to Paul, unbelievers "suppress the truth" because they do not want to believe the message of the Gospel. Their minds are "defiled" (Titus 1:5). In an exegesis of the text in Romans 1, the American theologian and Southern Baptist Convention leader, Albert Mohler, who *Time* magazine in 2003 called "the reigning intellectual of the evangelical movement in the U.S.,"[12] explains that "the knowledge crisis" for the atheist is not in what they "do not know" but rather in what they "will not know."[13]

That is once again not to say that Mohler or Paul is deny-

ing that any "unregenerate person" can solve diseases or per-
form well in algebra, but rather that when it comes to "the
most important issues of life and meaning" their reasoning is
"corrupted."[14] Once again, true knowledge for the Christian, the
kind that saves, the kind that matters, cannot be found separate
from God.

The Conundrum

This passage touches on a fascinating conundrum in the Bible.
Unbelievers are held accountable for their rejection of the Gospel because they do not have a valid excuse for not believing in
God (Rom 1:19). At the same time, the Bible says that the Gospel
is "veiled to those who are perishing" (2 Cor 4:3). It was because
of this that Jesus spoke to the Pharisees in parables "because seeing they do not see, and hearing they do not hear" (Mat 13:13).
The conundrum is, why would God hold people accountable for
truths that are veiled to them?

When reading Bible verses that seemingly contradict one
another in this fashion, unbelievers might rightly object that
the Bible is inconsistent and should thus be discarded as futile.
I would not be so quick to do so. Perhaps there is something to
learn in this seeming contradiction.

It is indeed confusing that unbelievers are held accountable for something they have not done. But this is the crux of
the Christian message. So, we cannot simply let it go. We are all
held accountable for the Fall of Adam and Eve – something we
have not done. It remains a mystery that God is currently punishing us for being born into a sinful condition that we did not
choose. No, free will is not a satisfactory answer to anyone who
has considered how little we genuinely choose in this world.
Adam and Eve decided to fall, and here we are, hundreds of thousands of years later, still being sent to hell for a choice we had no
hope to participate in.

Is God Unjust?

In Romans 9, one of the most philosophically interesting texts in the New Testament, Paul confronts the elephant in the room, so to speak, on whether there is "injustice on God's part" because of our discovered conundrum (Rom 9:14). In response to this, Paul writes:

> By no means! For he says to Moses, "I will have mercy on whom I have mercy, and I will have compassion on whom I have compassion." So then it depends not on human will or exertion, but on God, who has mercy. For the Scripture says to Pharaoh, "For this very purpose I have raised you up, that I might show my power in you, and that my name might be proclaimed in all the earth." So then he has mercy on whomever he wills, and he hardens whomever he wills.
>
> You will say to me then, "Why does he still find fault? For who can resist his will?" **But who are you, O man, to answer back to God?** Will what is molded say to its molder, "Why have you made me like this?" Has the potter no right over the clay, to make out of the same lump one vessel for honorable use and another for dishonorable use? What if God, desiring to show his wrath and to make known his power, has endured with much patience vessels of wrath prepared for destruction, in order to make known the riches of his glory for vessels of mercy, which he has prepared beforehand for glory— even us whom he has called, not from the Jews only but also from the Gentiles? Rom 9:14-24

In what right should we, as unbelievers, object to God? Here, the answer is not as straightforward as secular critics might argue. In the end, the Bible clearly blames unbelievers for their delusion; To remind you, Paul writes, "claiming to be wise" unbelievers became "fools" (Rom 1:22). If God is the Creator of the Universe, there is no way to object to His way, even if we find it "unjust." Thus, it very well may be the case that God's existence is veiled to every unbeliever, and that faith by grace is the only way to have the "knowledge" that the Bible celebrates.

The Nature of Salvation

This understanding of God and our relation to Him touches on the nature of salvation. Christian teaching is clear that reasoning alone will not persuade any unbeliever to Christ. You cannot be saved of your own volition – salvation is a gift from God (Eph 2:8). It is the believer's responsibility to preach and plant the seed, but it is on God to make the seed grow (1 Cor 3:6). Paul writes that his message and preaching "were not in persuasive words of wisdom, but in demonstration of the Spirit and of power, so that your faith would not rest on the wisdom of men, but on the power of God" (1 Cor 2:4-5).

However, when the Bible speaks of the "foolishness" of unbelievers, it does not praise the "wisdom" of Christians; Instead, it sets the stage for the crucial work of God in saving the sinner. There are seeming exceptions in the Bible where some are persuaded with "reasoning," but when we look deeper into these cases, it is clear that God gets the credit. The believers gladly give it, acknowledging their unwillingness to believe. For example, in Acts 19:8-9, some in Thessalonica "were persuaded" and were brought to Christ as a result. This, as is explained in 2 Corinthians 4:4-6, is both the result of God's work (verse 6) and Paul's teaching or rather Paul's "proclaiming of Jesus as Lord" (verse 5).

As I hope to have shown above, the fact that the wisdom of the world is foolishness to God does not excuse Christians feeling morally and intellectually superior over their unbelieving neighbors. Paul repeatedly writes on the importance of boasting in Christ rather than in oneself. In one such passage, he argues:

> But whatever anyone else dares to boast of—*I am speaking as a fool*—I also dare to boast of that. Are they Hebrews? So am I. Are they Israelites? So am I.

Are they offspring of Abraham? So am I. Are they servants of Christ? I am a better one—*I am talking like a madman*—with far greater labors, far more imprisonments, with countless beatings, and often near death. Five times I received at the hands of the Jews the forty lashes less one. ... And, apart from other things, there is the daily pressure on me of my anxiety for all the churches. Who is weak, and I am not weak? Who is made to fall, and I am not indignant?

If I must boast, I will boast of the things that show my weakness. 2 Cor 11:21-30

Historically, of course, the teaching of Christian exemption resulted in all sorts of unethical implications. The already mentioned writer, Jacoby, explains that one of the church founders and Christianity's most influential intellectuals, Augustine, "essentially believed that a people so foolish and evil as to refuse the truth claim of Christianity deserved almost every other form of abuse."[15] It is not hard to see the logical connection between the Bible and Augustine's harsh admonishments. Others that instill this hostile belief toward unbelievers forget that the ability to understand the Bible and have faith cannot be earned but is a gift. The idea that irrationality and separation with God are so entrenched within us is not unique to early Christian writers, however. Many Christian leaders today argue in a similar way that unbelievers are somehow uniquely responsible for their unbelief. Grudem, for example, writes:

[A] Christian view understands that some of the evil in people's hearts is so irrational that it cannot be restrained by reasoning but only by force.[16]

Reasoning and Humility
Biblically, the notion that "true" wisdom, or knowledge that saves, comes from God should implant humility within the Christian. Then, we could say that there is some good in it. For, if your faith is not your own, you have nothing to boast about (Gal

6:14). As much as Christians are called to "explain" and "prove" or to "give answers" and "be prepared," the result is entirely on the workings of God. Otherwise, salvation would rest on the ability to reason well, and that does not seem like the grace and faith that Paul often calls for in the Christian's life. And, more importantly, that would damn a good percentage of the population.

Look around. Not everyone is inclined to think about biblical issues or Jesus. Some are born without any aptitude for thinking about moral, let alone biblical matters. That is not because they are "sinful," although some Christian thinkers would like you to think so. Instead, it is because these "sinners" have a natural tendency toward other things than reading and writing. Biblical knowledge comes hand in hand with a willingness to analyze texts. It would seem unfair and borderline unethical to develop a religion that rewards behavior that cannot be trained or instilled in us. Biblically, acting on your faith with renewed acts seems more critical than merely reasoning about the Bible. Otherwise, Jesus would have told the Pharisees to "think more" rather than to "believe," "have faith," and "be humble."

Christians and Thought

So, our intellectual capacity to reason well is not necessary for salvation because otherwise, salvation would be based on works, something that is fundamentally at odds with Christian teaching.

There is a large divide between Christian thinkers that put too much of an emphasis on understanding the Word of God over thinkers that stress a relationship with Christ, thinking that the two are exclusive. Of course, they are not. More liberal Christians believe that those that dwell on God's attributes from the Bible too much are reminiscent of the Pharisees in the New Testament that Jesus slanders and condemns repeatedly. That is a misconception, however. Piper writes that "If [Christians] abandon thinking, [Christians] abandon the Bible, and if [Christians] abandon the Bible, [they] abandon God."[17] Piper quotes Ephesians 3:3-4 in support of this claim, where Paul writes, in verse 4 that "When you read this, you can perceive my insight into the mystery of Christ." Paul is implying here that the act of reading gives "insight" into Christ.

Liberal Christians wrongly think that prioritizing 'knowing God' is contrary to 'loving God.' The commandments in the Bible to reason well and explain and prove are certainly less important than the ones concerning saving faith and the fruit of the Spirit. However, that does not discredit the importance of biblical teaching. Paul acknowledges that the Church body is composed of different "parts" (1 Cor 12:12). Each Church member is given different spiritual gifts, some in prophecy, some in speaking in tongues, and some in biblical teaching (Rom 12:6-7). The Church thus relies on one another. But when it comes to knowing Scripture and dwelling on it, Jesus is transparent in His call to believers: "If you abide in me, and my words abide in you, ask whatever you wish, and it will be done for you" (John 15:7).

There is no sure way to admonish abiding in Jesus' words or "explaining" and "proving" in the Christian's life. Jesus calls for His followers to "abide" in His Word, but we do not have a detailed explanation of what that would look like or what it even means. Should Christians be memorizing Scripture every day? To what extent should Christians explain and prove their beliefs to unbelievers, for example? How often? Would it be daily or bi-weekly or bi-monthly? Or is it only when the Christian is asked about their faith that they should explain Christian teaching to the unbeliever? We stumble into some difficulties.

Reasoning, Morality, and Christian Behavior

That being said, if you, as a sincere Christian, have not once read the Bible and rely on others for your understanding of God, you are not doing your duty as a believer. That is not to say that your faith depends on works, but rather that you should bear fruit (John 15:5). Otherwise, you are simply not a Christian. Yes, "abiding" in Jesus' words, whatever that means for Jesus, implies that you keep His commandments, as that is what follows in the following verses in John 15 (particularly John 15:10). In the end, Jesus cursed the fig tree (Mark 11:12-25) and "spits" out the lukewarm believer (Rev 3:16). And so it should concern you whether you are following His commandments.

We can see these admonishments against lukewarm behavior throughout the Bible; There is a holiness without which a Christian will not see the Lord (Hebrews 12:14). I am not implying that moral behavior is a gatekeeper to heaven; The gatekeeper is saving faith in Jesus. Instead, moral behavior is the direct result of this saving faith. Paul urges the Galatians to avoid sexual immorality, impurity, sensuality, strife, jealousy, drunkenness, orgies, and the like because those who "do such things will not inherit the kingdom of God" (Galatians 5:19-21). Of course, Paul is not saying that avoiding these acts alone will guarantee someone a place in heaven, as any Christian will readily recognize. When Jesus calls for "perfection" from His followers, He is more suggesting that they rely on His perfection, rather than be perfect themselves (Mat 5:48).

As much as Christians rely on reasoning, they know that that is not where Christianity's argument ends. So, Peter calls for good behavior among the Gentiles so they "see [their] good deeds and glorify God" (1 Peter 2:12). The Christian apologist, Ravi Zacharias, recognized this and urged Christians to behave biblically to prove the truthfulness of their saving faith. Zacharias writes that "The greatest obstacle to the impact of the gospel has not been its inability to provide answers, but the failure on our part to live it out."[18]

Unfortunately, Christians today are not typically marked by their difference from "the World." Research suggests that the behavior of Christians is no different than that of atheists when it comes to materialism and the poor, domestic violence in marriage, divorce rates, pornography-usage, and racism.[19] How are they then to persuade the rest of society of the truthfulness of their faith? Yes, the Christian must be committed to reasoning, but, importantly, they must also bear fruit and live out the

Gospel they dwell on.

The Christian Message is Not Wise or Pleasant

The strength of the Christian argument was never meant to persuade unbelievers, only God can do that. This makes the job of Christian apologists tricky. Unbelievers are compared to "lawlessness" and "darkness" in the Bible, whereas Christians are compared to God's chosen people of Israel (2 Cor 6:14-15). The unbelieving in Revelations are included in a long list that includes "the cowardly," the "abominable," "murderers," "sorcerers," and "idolaters" (Rev 21:8). Their place is in a "lake that burns with fire and brimstone" (Rev 21:8). When Paul preached the Gospel, he was shouted at (Acts 21:36), lashed (2 Cor 11:24), and even stoned to the point that observers thought he was dead (Acts 14:19). Initially, the Gospel was not a very pleasant message, which is why it is surprising we have made it so today.

Apart from the message of the Gospel not being pleasant, it is also not intellectually compelling. Indeed, it would not be an understatement to say that you would be unbiblical to claim that the Christian message was wise. If you are a Christian, you should not be surprised that "the World" rejects your beliefs. You believe that God's Son came and died for your sins 2,000 years ago on what Roman soldiers crucified criminals on. The Bible's repeated calls against unbelievers and dismissal of them were never meant to be "tolerant" because they were never meant to persuade unbelievers. Only the saving work of Christ can do that. Even Jesus Himself expected "the world" to hate Christians. Why would Christians today think otherwise?

> If the world hates you, know that it has hated me before it hated you. If you were of the world, the world would love you as its own; but because you are not of the world, but I chose you out of the world, therefore the world hates you. John 15:18-19

The Bible clearly teaches that unbelievers are restricted in their ability to reason about intellectual and moral issues;

they suppress the truth because of their sinfulness, disobedience, and arrogance. According to Paul, God has ultimately revealed himself through nature, making his existence undeniable. However, this truth is simultaneously veiled to unbelievers. So, unbelievers are both denied the "knowledge that saves" and punished for not accepting it.

Religious intolerance is now marked by incessant indifference to those that disagree with them. Suppose these intolerant Christians take the teaching of Scripture seriously, which, if they identify as Christians, they should, then they must be patient. I cannot imagine Paul's admonishment to reason, explain and prove, to mean anything other than patiently elaborating on beliefs to effectively persuade others (Acts 17:2-3). The name-calling and classifying that happens far too often in discourse today is surely not what Paul had in mind. As we saw from earlier on in this chapter, John writes that Christians should be known for their love, which, he argues, will persuade others of the Christian message (John 13:34-35). Many Christians will fail to do so because they are sinners. Nonetheless, the commandment is clear.

All in all, it seems that Christian teaching is not opposed to reasoning at all. Indeed, the Bible urges reasoning again and again. The problem is that the Bible also calls for other things, and it is challenging to discern the highest priority. In the last chapter of this book, I will explore what could be the largest priority in the Christian's life. For now, this should suffice. The "Age of Unreason," that Jacoby spoke of, may be met by Christians who stick to the Bible's call to reason well, explain and prove, set themselves apart from the World, discern, defend and confirm, and be prepared to answer questions regarding their beliefs. But they should not be surprised when atheists reject these beliefs.

Chapter 2

Atheism
& an Age of Unreason

What is there for an atheist to think about? Since atheists reject the existence of God, why should they think about anything in the first place? What's the point of it all? There is no afterlife – just darkness when we die. Christians can think about God because it can result in a better relationship with Him, the Creator of the Universe. They can find fulfillment and meaning in that assurance. Atheists, Christians claim, have a more difficult time defending a meaningful or thoughtful life. Our thoughts are an accident, the random by-product of evolution, they insist. So how will atheists deal with the ubiquitous "Age of Unreason" that Jacoby spoke of in the previous chapter?

Atheists are able to justify some thinking, at least. We could say that the purpose of science and medicine is to understand ourselves and other species better and reduce suffering. So, at least thinking medically has some function. But what are we to do with thinking about philosophical issues? Christians may claim that an atheist has no reason to get up in the morning, let alone pick up Dostoevsky, Dickens, or any other writer, for their reading pleasure. If there is no meaning to life apart from God and no real satisfaction in life apart from dwelling on God, then it could be argued that there truly is no reason for the atheist to think about anything. Why not just drink, be merry, sleep around, and so forth, as Christians tell us to. It certainly sounds ... fun?

Let me try to do my best to defend that atheists do have something to think about and can be very happy doing so. Although, my argument in this chapter is based more in history than the previous chapter. I will also point out where reason fails us and why our intuitions often prevail over reason.

Atheism Grows

Studies show that the more educated a country becomes, the more secular it becomes. Atheism, as a worldview, is growing at exponential rates in the United States, what was previously thought of as a rather Christian nation. In the 1950s, less than 5 percent of Americans identified as atheists. That number barely grew toward the end of the century, to only 8 percent in the 1990s. In 2001, that number increased more steadily to 14 percent. Then in 2010, to 16 percent. In 2013, to 19 percent. Some of the latest national surveys suggest that the number is up to 30 percent, which means that atheism would officially be the largest worldview in America.[1] The United States is not alone in becoming more secular, however. In my home country, Canada, at the beginning of the 19th-century, 2 percent of Canadians claimed not to be religious. That number has grown to more than 30 percent.[2] The same trend applies to most developed countries, including Australia, Holland, Great Britain, the Scandinavian countries, the Czech Republic, France, Belgium, Germany, etc.

With the steady rise of atheism across the West, should we expect a complete abandonment of reason and logical thinking that is repeatedly condoned and urged in the Bible, as we saw in the previous chapter? I would like to think not. In fact, I think we have good reason to believe that even an atheist can urge people to appreciate reasoning in their personal lives. The connection between atheism and reasoning, however, is obviously not necessary. We should not predict that society will be better off without religion automatically. As with most things, the answer is not entirely clear. The research can direct us in both directions.

Psychologists Ralph Wood, Peter Hill, and Bernard Spilka write based on decades of research that, yes, "As a broad generalization, the more religious an individual is, the more prejudiced that person is."[3] The former Duke University Professor, Deborah Hall, compared fifty-five studies on the relationship between racism and religion in America and found that religious people tend to be more racist.[4] And the sociologist, Phil Zuckerman, writes in *Living the Secular Life*, that religious people are more likely to be vengeful, nationalistic, and militaristic. On the other hand, secular people are more likely to be tolerant and believe in global warming, for example.[5] Despite these findings, we should not be quick to dismiss the Christian defense of reasoning. Since these studies very well may be instances of correlation rather than causation.

The Development of Reason

In the West, most of our discussions concerning morality, reason, and the natural sciences originated with those we call the "pre-Socratics," the ones that preceded Socrates, more than 2,000 years ago in Ancient Greece. The thinkers most known from this period include Thale, Anaxagoras, Democritus, and Pythagoras. The pre-Socratics are responsible for several important developments in geometry, mathematics, and astronomy, to name but a few fields of interest. Of course, similar conversations and work was being done elsewhere as well.

Many societies, for example, had utilized their understanding of astronomy to be able to manage the open seas, architecture to construct wondrous monuments like the Pyramids in Ancient Egypt, and typography or oratory to settle moral and political disputes, as was the case with Cleon and Brasidas infamously recounted by the Ancient Greek historian, Thucydides. Our ancestors were by no means clueless.

The most influential thinkers following the pre-Socratics in Ancient Greece were Socrates and his most formidable pupil, Plato. These two thinkers obsessively thought about living properly in society. Indeed when speaking of Socrates, the philosopher Anthony Gottlieb, writes that "No other great philosopher has been so obsessed with righteous living."[6] Socrates did not shy away from criticism and obsessively argued with those he disagreed with, popularizing the "Socratic method," an argumentative questioning technique used by lawyers in court to this day.

In fact, Ancient Greeks held that criticism could be among the best uses for speech.[7] Among the most important aspects of speech and its prevalence in Ancient Greece was that it could be written down. Alphabetic writing was first seen in Greece around the 8th century BCE and became common-use by the 6th century BCE.[8] This was important, of course, because texts are more easily scrutinized than speech, allowing for thinking to develop and expand on one another similar to peer-review in academia. Without criticism, thought would remain unchallenged without hope for improvement.

The Influence of the Greeks

The influence of the Ancient Greeks was long and far-reaching. Indeed, Plato could be considered one of the first popular intellectuals of the West. In his book, *The Dream of Reason*, Gottlieb writes that up unto the medieval era, "Whatever people believed, they believed because of Plato."[9] The philosopher, Bertrand Russell, says that "All philosophy is footnotes to Plato," which can be seen as an exaggeration but has some truth to it according to scholarly commentators.[10] Socrates and Plato both thought that virtue was intimately connected with knowledge.[11] Plato indeed passed down what became a Christian notion, that the senses deceive and that "objects of genuine knowledge" must be "eternal, perfect, [and] unchanging."[12]

Christians will perhaps notice the similarities between their own and Plato's view on knowledge because Augustine and most other Christian thinkers up until Aquinas adopted

Plato's philosophy into Christian doctrine that roman-catholics still profess today. Augustine wrote that "There are none who come nearer to us than the Platonists" and that "If these men could have had this life over again with us ... [t]hey would have become Christians, with the change of a few words and statements."[13]

The Church, however, was divided on which great philosopher they liked more. One of Christendom's most influential figures, Thomas Aquinas, gave more credence to Plato's brightest student, Aristotle, who happened to disagree with Plato on most of his views. The philosopher, A. C. Grayling writes that much of Aquinas' philosophy was a "straightforward adoption from Aristotle" whether that was concerning time, cosmology, perception, ethics, and the material world and God's relation to it.[14] It was clear that these philosophers were doing more than the early Church founders, who thought that the only noteworthy thing to know about this world was that God created it.[15]

Aristotle believed that a contemplative life is the "best life."[16] And his life certainly shows that he lived up to what he preached. Aristotle's work consists of almost one and a half million words. There is also good reason to think that this is no more than a quarter of his actual work because we have only managed to preserve his lecture notes from antiquity. These include books on topics such as ethics, political theory, rhetoric, poetry, constitutional history, theology, zoology, meteorology, astronomy, physics, chemistry, the scientific method, anatomy, the foundations of mathematics, language, formal logic, techniques of reasoning, fallacies, household management, mechanics, among other subjects. Two of his contributions stand above all the rest because of the preservation of their original nature and influence: formal logic, which Aristotle invented without any apparent influence, and biology, in which he was referenced until Charles Darwin developed his theory for natural selection in the 19th century.[17] Aristotle was one of the original polymaths and broadly contributed to most fields.

We may be impressed by all of Aristotle's achievements, but the educated people of the late medieval times, in Gottlieb's words, "ate, drank and breathed him."[18] Dante (1265-1321) referred to Aristotle in his *Divine Comedy* as "the master of those who know."[19] Aquinas would merely describe Aristotle as 'the Philosopher.' Later Rene Descartes envied his popularity and said, "How fortunate that man was: whatever he wrote, whether he gave it much thought or not, is regarded by most people today as having oracular authority."[20]

Aristotle's books are not easy to read, as with any classical work of philosophy, but they follow the same structure and form of logic academics use today. Gottlieb even suggests that Aristotle "writes like a modern-day professor" because "today's academics are direct descendants of a line that dutifully copied his approach."[21] However, some grew to dislike Aristotle because he was the juxtaposition of Plato, whose views were more in line with Christian dogma.

Aristotle had a uniquely different view from Plato (and hence Christians) on both the metaphysical and physical world. Aristotle believed that the soul dies after death; Christians believed the soul was eternal. Aristotle believed that the world had always existed; Christians said that it had a beginning. Aristotle's God was deistic; Christians believed that God cared for them to the point of sacrificing His own Son. This is why many Christians, apart from some exceptions, dismissed Aristotle's contributions and strayed from Greek thought — mistakenly so.[22]

The Renaissance

It is argued that by the year 1000 in Europe, almost all branches of knowledge from medicine and biology to physics and astronomy had "virtually collapsed."[23] Even the Christian monks who were acquiring knowledge in the monasteries knew significantly less than the Greeks, who preceded them by eight centuries. Meanwhile, the Muslim world was making rapid progress in medicine, science, mathematics, and philosophy, ever since Muslim scholars began translating Greek works (namely from Aristotle and Plato) into Syriac and Arabic.[24] Aristotle's mark was made on the world.

After more than 1,000 years of near-total silence from all of these disciplines, the Renaissance ushered in an era of intellectual curiosity reminiscent of the Greeks. The "humanist" movement of the Renaissance refocused scholarly attention on a study of ethics and politics.[25] These humanists emphasized a teaching in literature, philology, oratory, history, among other things, which helped young men prepare for work in councils, city tribunals, and Papal offices.[26]

Notably, many Renaissance humanists were Christians since an atheist life, where you deny the existence of any gods, was unfathomable at the time. So many Renaissance thinkers can be seen making attempts to reconcile moral philosophy with Christain doctrine.[27] However, their writing indicates a more deistic understanding of the Universe and resembles little of what we think of as Christianity today. Instead, we see that Renaissance thinkers were slowly abandoning superstition and emphasizing empirical observations over *a priori* convictions.

This period of philosophy gave us what are thought to be the two founders of modern philosophy: Rene Descartes and Francis Bacon. Most importantly, Bacon introduced a novel methodological enterprise for knowledge that stressed empirical thought over divine revelation, and Descartes contributed to epistemology with "Cartesian Skepticism," among other things, guaranteeing him fame in philosophy classes across the world to this day.[28] In this period, philosophers started adopting the concept of the individual into their thinking, abandoning the Christian collective notion of the Church.

In his book *The Order of Things,* an epistemological work that traces the classification of knowledge from modernism to the present, the postmodern philosopher Michel Foucault discusses this development of thought from collectivism to individualism. To illustrate it, he describes the reclassification of thought in the infamous painting, titled "Las Meninas," by the Spanish painter Velazquez. The portrait shows the Spanish royal court, featuring King Philip the IV, Margaret Theresa, and several other notable royal figures. For Foucault, Velazquez's painting exemplifies the pivotal shift seen in humanist thought around the time of the Renaissance.

In the painting, the reflection in the mirror seems to be that of the King and Queen. Upon further reflection, it becomes more apparent that Velazquez is painting us, the observers. With this, Foucault argues, Velazquez shows that a space that was once "privileged" and "inescapable," meant only for royalty, was shifting into a space meant for everyone.[29] The Spanish court in the painting becomes the one that is "most ignored" since the King and Queen are in view but not the focus of attention.[30] Foucault thus helpfully defines the origin of humanist thought, where the subject (the individual) becomes the object of focus.[31] This is an important distinction. Before this point, society was mostly collectivist, and now it was becoming more subjective, individualistic, and interpretative.

The Enlightenment

Enlightenment philosophers drew on this new classification, recognizing the importance of the individual and what many called the 'dignity of man.' In contrast to the traditional Christian view of humans as fallen creatures unable to redeem themselves, a view to which even the most rational and optimistic believers such as Aquinas and Dante subscribed, humanists saw themselves as self-creating agents, free to transform themselves and the world through their actions.

Few would deny that the largely secular Enlightenment had abandoned Christian reasoning as authoritative. The philosopher, Baruch Spinoza, was among the first to argue that the Bible is inconsistent, which led many to consider the possibility that God's Word is not inspired by God but written by regular people.[32]

Indeed, the historian Jonathan Israel argues that "during the century 1650-1750 [no one] remotely rivaled Spinoza's notoriety, as the chief challenger of the fundamentals of revealed religion, received ideas, tradition, morality and what was everywhere regarded . . . as divinely constituted political authority."[33] Spinoza still thought of Jesus as morally exemplary, but he did not think so because of His deity.[34] Gottlieb writes that the "religion" of Spinoza was "rather close to modern secularism."[35]

After Spinoza, Bayle proclaimed in *Various Thoughts on the Occasion of a Comet* that atheist societies may not necessarily be immoral societies as was widely believed at the time of writing.[36] Philosophers across the Enlightenment continued to inspire each other, resulting in much advancement in intellectual insight, whether in the natural sciences, or philosophy and political theory. When Jeremy Bentham, for example, read the Scottish philosopher David Hume's work on morality, he claimed that he "felt as if scales had fallen from [his] eyes."[37] I point out this inspiration and influence because reasoning is often celebrated throughout history for its own sake. It seems that secular people are fully capable of celebrating reason and promoting its use in society.

On the other hand, protestant thinkers like Martin Luther and John Calvin rejected the working of human reason. Malik explains that for them, "[H]uman reason was too weak to comprehend God's plan."[38] As I expanded on in the previous chapter, God's ways are mysterious, and His will is both undeniable and difficult to understand.

In fact, Luther thought that Aquinas' incessant focus on Aristotle and his attempt to reconcile faith and reason was his most unforgivable fault. Biblically, reason can only help humans up to a point; Reason cannot save or redeem sinners. Malik explains that "The Reformation was an intensely conservative religious reaction against the spirit of reason that Aquinas had introduced into Christianity."[39]

With the rise of the concept of the individual, many

were given the freedom to think for themselves and reject established dogma, both Aristotelian and religious.[40] Of course, Christians will once again like to take credit for the development of the idea of the individual, because, as they argue, God put value into every soul (Gen 1:27). However, throughout Christendom, that teaching was not as inclusive as Christians think of it today. On the contrary, some could argue that Luther and Calvin, the fathers of Protestantism, changed the world for the worse, namely in that they reinforced a level of anti-semitism comparable to that found in Adolf Hitler's *Mein Kempf*. I would not go so far, but it is something that scholars will endlessly argue over.

The Fulfilment Knowledge Provides

Many of these thinkers from Plato to Hume have found it fulfilling to ponder about the meaning of life and the world's philosophical underpinnings while among us. History shows that we do not necessarily need Christianity to justify thinking. Often, an absence of faith does not lead to despair in reasoning, but rather a desire for compelling answers to interesting questions. Each one of us can appreciate answering deep probing questions that taunt us late at night and deep into the morning.

In my view, it is not an exaggeration to suggest that the connection between nihilism and secular thought is devoid of any substance. I will discuss that further in the chapter on The Meaning of Life & the Atheist. For those interested in some of the deep questions of life and meaning that I've been discussing in these chapters, we feel immense gratitude to the writers we read. As C. S. Lewis put it in one of my favorite passages written on what we owe to writers:

> Those of us who have been true readers all our life seldom realize the enormous extension of our being that we owe to authors. We realize it best when we talk with an unliterary friend. He may be full of goodness and good sense, but he inhabits a tiny world. In it,

we should be suffocated. My own eyes are not enough for me. ...in reading great literature I become a thousand men and yet remain myself. Like the night sky in the Greek poem, I see with a myriad of eyes, but it is still I who see. Here, as in worship, in love, in moral action, and in knowing, I transcend myself; and am never more myself than when I do.— *An Experiment in Criticism*

Throughout history, many have identified with the sentiment behind Lewis' words. It is incorrect to think that people cannot reason because they do not have God in their lives, the same way as it would be to suggest that we cannot behave morally because we do not have God in our lives. History simply testifies to the fact that independence in thinking from established dogma was a prized and celebrated achievement. There are, however, apparent limits to knowledge.

I want to make sure that I am not propagating that reason guides us above all else and that atheism is naturally more superior to religious thinking. In fact, there is research that suggests that intuitive thinking is much more prominent in politics and philosophy than we might think. Intuition takes up much of our ability to reason well about important issues.

For now, I want to delve deeper into the intuitions we have about society and why reason alone cannot save us. This point is perhaps one where Christians and atheists will agree on, apart from Christianity's persuasion that the most real knowledge available, "the knowledge that saves" that I mentioned in the previous chapter, is only attainable by those who believe in God. That should also be held to scrutiny.

The Limits to Knowledge
We think of ourselves as purely rational thinkers when we frequently replace one logical fallacy for the next. When it comes to our feelings of moral superiority, for example, one might think that those who think about these issues the most are cer-

tainly the more moral ones. Some interesting research into this testifies to why that is not a necessary connection.

One such study, conducted by the philosopher Eric Schwitzgebel, showed that moral philosophers do not behave in a more moral way than other philosophy professors and professors in general. Schwitzgebel's findings show that moral philosophers are not more likely to give to charity, vote, call their mothers, donate blood or organs, clean up after themselves at conferences, and respond to emails from students than other professors.[41] This is significant because it suggests that moral reasoning alone does not make people better. There is something more to our moral behavior; In the end, our thinking about these issues is never enough.

There are many things we get wrong in society, and we seem to do so collectively. The public policy analyst Bobby Duffy beautifully explores this conundrum in *Why We're Nearly Wrong About Nearly Everything*. One potent example he uses is how the public answers the question 'Is the Great Wall of China visible from outer space?'

His findings suggest that about a half of people think that the Great Wall of China can be seen from space, when, in fact, it is not.[42] The reason why so many believe in these, upon later reflection, blatant falsities are numerous. For one, Duffy writes, this question is probably something you have not thought about a lot. Secondly, you could have heard the answer to the question from someone when not focusing on the claim, which became an instilled memory. Lastly, you may have come up with the answer quickly, because you wanted to continue with your life since you did not think it was important.[43]

There may be many reasons for thinking so, but the obvious answer is that if you knew basic facts about the Great Wall of China, you would never think to answer the question with a 'yes.' This would be relatively easy to prove, writes Duffy. And it is. In the first place, the length of the Great Wall of China, what we instinctively think is what makes it relevant to see it from space, does not make it visible from space. The width would be responsible for that. The fact that we get tedious questions like the one above wrong is not the issue; problems arise when we answer political and social questions with the same certainty.

Intuition and Intelligence

There are clear limitations to each of us in our biases and how we reason. So, it would be unfair to say that atheists are naturally smarter than Christians simply because they believe they only accept claims based on empirical evidence and not faith. Dawkins, for example, argues that "We should always be open-minded, but the only good reason to believe that something exists is if there is real evidence that it does."[44]

Unfortunately, it is not as simple as Dawkins suggests. The "evidence" that each camp thinks is correct is highly disputed. N. T. Wright and other New Testament Christian scholars would argue that there is plenty of "evidence" for Jesus' resurrection, for example. Others, however, will disagree and say that there is plenty of evidence that the Bible is erroneous. So, this is clearly a matter of epistemology. We need to agree on reality before we decide on how we assess evidence.

The philosopher Jurgen Habermas, for instance, argued that "Religion cannot be characterized simply as irrational; reason has its limits; and the 'scientific' belief that science will give us a new self-understanding is, moreover, bad philosophy."[45] I would not go so far as the New Atheists have and say that Christian scholars are especially deluded. In the end, we are all deluded in many ways; we cannot see the faults in our reasoning. Not even the smartest among us are aware of their own biases and errors.

Indeed, studies conducted by Keith Stanovich show that people with higher IQ are as susceptible as the rest of us to cognitive bias, coining the term "dysrationalia" for those that can reason well but fail to in key moments.[46] The difference between intelligent people and less intelligent people exposed to cognitive bias is only in that when you tell the more intelligent person they are wrong, they are more likely to show where they made the cognitive mistake.[47]

Thus, intelligence is not the sole predictor of how often we are correct and how often we take the counsel of our intuitive beliefs over rational judgments. The French cognitive scientists Hugo Mercier and Dan Sperber similarly found upon reviewing the literature on motivated reasoning that "skilled arguers . . . are not after the truth but after arguments supporting their views."[48] Even the most intelligent are susceptible to the fundamental errors that uneducated minds make.

Indeed, the central value of an education, Stanovich points out, is to "attempt to develop controlled processing styles that override the fundamental computational bias and thus enable learned rule systems to operate on decoupled presentations."[49] Stanovich, along with others, argues that the "fundamental computational bias" that each one of us applies, without exception, is our first instinctual reaction to cognitive problems. That is why we are often incorrect in our judgments. Our "slow thinking," or rational thinking, is reserved for when other options have already been exhausted.[50]

Stanovich has further argued that we do not take this irrationality seriously in society and romanticize high IQ to our fault, meaning that our society is often led by people who are incapable of second-guessing their views since they are considered intelligent.[51] This can be exemplified by the former U.S. President George W. Bush, whose university performance could testify to higher intelligence. Because of this, one could think that Bush would make educated directions when it came to policy and foreign relations. Instead, Bush's decisions were repeatedly based on his "gut feeling."

When meeting the Russian President, Vladimir Putin, for example, Bush claimed that upon "looking [Putin] in the eye" he got a sense that he could trust him, which turned out to be remarkably false. While in Office, Bush showed a staggering lack of intellectual curiosity about things he knew little about and quite literally prayed to God for guidance, which Joseph Heath explains is "just a way of bolstering support for one's gut feelings" since it is uniquely difficult to discern what is God's will and what is your own will.[52]

Is Religion Irrational?

Religion may not be entirely irrational, although many of its beliefs rely on several fallacies and cognitive errors. Cognitive psychologists expand on some of these errors, which we are all susceptible to. Among the most common, for example, is *Belief bias*, where we classify an argument as illogical that only differs from our view in conclusion, not in structural form. One example that shows this bias is with those who accept the divinity of Christ solely because the "Bible says so," and then reject Allah's divinity simply because the "Koran says so" (and they disagree with the Koran without knowing why). In other words, when presented with identical argument forms that replace the term "Jesus Christ" with "Allah," they reject the argument.[53] We often reject arguments without knowing why simply because they differ with our conclusions in similar ways.

Cognitive biases and their prevalence are disheartening and may lead some of us to despair, especially because everyone professes certainty. Heath writes that one of the most well-established claims in the literature on cognitive bias is that "people are terrible at distinguishing genuine irrationality from simple disagreement."[54] The cognitive psychologist Jonathan Haidt explores this in more depth in his book, *The Righteous Mind: Why Good People Are Divided by Religion and Politics*.

In his book, Haidt, a self-proclaimed intuitionist, argues that "we must be wary of any *individual's* ability to reason."[55] He writes that our Western tendency to worship reason above all else is "itself an illustration of one of the most long-lived delusions in Western history."[56] He argues that from Plato to Kant and Kohlberg, rationalists attributed reasoning with moral behavior, which has been proven to be a somewhat false correlation, as was shown above.[57]

Haidt uses an analogy of the Elephant and the Rider in his book *The Happiness Hypothesis*. He compares our emotional side, the intuitive, fast thinker, with the Elephant and the rational side, or slow thinker, with the Rider. When in disagreement with your emotional side, Haidt points out the obvious that the Elephant will overrule the decision of the Rider. We can all recount countless stories when this happens in our personal lives, from when we are stuck in traffic, to the slightest inconvenience, such as someone cutting the grocery line, or when we fight with our partners over insignificant things. We are all guilty of the Elephant overcoming our better nature. When it comes to broader questions, such as those that we are exploring in this book, we are all susceptible to fast thinking, which is far more problematic.

Repetition, Stories, and Our Biases

One of the other key components to making a complex political or moral issue trigger our fast thinking is by being exposed to *repetition* throughout our lives. This allows for some stories instilled within us from early childhood, such as religious stories, to take a strong foothold in our lives, making them more challenging to abandon later on. They are difficult to dispose of because we forget why we believe them in the first place, as was shown with the example of the question concerning whether the Great Wall of China can be seen from Space. Indeed, the theory behind repetition is considered to be a well-documented theory in experimental psychology:

> The more time one is exposed to a particular statement, the more one is likely to believe the statement to be true. This relationship between repetition and perceived truth is mediated by familiarity; repetition increases and, in turn, familiarity is used as a heuristic for determining the truth of a statement.[58]

Yuval Noah Harari popularized the notion of successful narratives, such as money, nationalism, and religion, that are most commonly used across societies, in his book *Sapiens: A Brief History of Humankind*. Harari points out that many throughout history sacrificed themselves for the "greater good" because of these narratives. This can be seen from the United States and the USSR during the Cold War but, really, from any nationalistic society (which includes pretty much all of them). As a species, believing in stories arguably helped our survival; We needed unity when there was very little to agree upon.

Therefore, repetition is a common effective way to manipulate society. Politicians are perhaps most known for purposefully planting false notions into the public for personal gain. One particularly amusing exchange that exemplifies repetition used in politics was between Sarah Palin on *The Today Show* with Matt Lauer, on April 2, 2012. When commenting about Obama's first term as President, Palin claimed that Obama failed the country with his "socialist policies" and that any Republican nominee would be better than Obama. After a few minutes of conversation, Palin was asked whether the economy was improving at all, to which she replied, "Maybe for some on Wall Street, but not for the millions still unemployed."[59]

Many noticed the apparent contradiction between Palin's two answers, the "socialist policies" and helping people on Wall Street get richer because, well, they are light and day. Heath uses this example to illustrate a point and helpfully explains that Palin's supposed contradiction was purposeful. The term "failed socialist policies" was regularly used at the time by conservative political commentators to reinforce the agenda that socialism is necessarily related to a failed state and Obama's first term.[60] It did not matter whether Obama ever indeed resembled a socialist state or even what they meant by socialism in the first place; What mattered was whether they instilled a false notion via repetition to influence the outcome of an election.

Slow Thinking

What is the solution to all of our intuitions, cognitive biases, and erroneous rationalizations? The authors I've been quoting in this chapter address some. The clearest is deliberate slow thinking. We need to stop ourselves when we hear something that triggers our emotional responses and pause. Then we need to read, converse with others (especially those we disagree with), and represent the counter-argument in its best form.

The philosopher Donald Davidson, whom I mentioned in my introduction, popularized this argument, claiming that we should always attempt to represent the opposing argument in a way that the other side would agree with. Some have even coined a term to describe this: to "steel-man" an argument, instead of "straw-man." I hope to have lived up to that goal in this chapter and the rest of the book.

Doing so is not glamorous, and few of us will be able to commit to this consistently. Nonetheless, it is something that we must do if we are to, in the words of Heath, "restore sanity" into our everyday lives.

Throughout history, reasoning was commonplace – even in places that rejected religious dogma and divine revelation. Many have found it deeply worthwhile to ponder on how the world works and have expressed their ideas on pen and paper for us to marvel at. We are all indebted to the thinkers that risked their lives to promote counter-cultural thinking. However, with this celebration of reason and intellectuals, I have also shown that reason is not the be-all and end-all. Countless studies are increasingly showing that our intuitive thinking clouds our judgment more often than we would like to admit. That does not defeat the purpose of reason. Instead, it reminds us that as humans, we are limited in our ability to remain unbiased. For good reason, this should humble us and help us in our attempt of dismissing the shackles of unfalsifiable dogma, religious or otherwise, in our own lives.

Chapter 3

Christianity & Moral Insight

Blessed is the man who walks not in the counsel of the wicked, nor stands in the way of sinners, nor sits in the seat of scoffers; but his delight is in the law of the lord, and on his law he meditates day and night. Ps. 1:1-2

When Jesus was asked what the greatest commandment was, he said that the entire Old Testament, both the Law and the Prophets, can be summarized in the following two commandments: (1) love God with all your heart, soul, and mind, and (2) love your neighbor as yourself (Matthew 22:36-40). There's much more to Christian ethics than loving God and loving your neighbor, however. The Bible is full of commandments, but for Jesus, these two are the most important since from them, the rest necessarily follow. That is not to deny that secular philosophy cannot help guide Christians toward ethical behavior but rather that Scripture is the main authority for Christian ethics.

Considering these two commandments, it may come as a surprise to any reader of history that Christendom has such a bad record at behaving morally. It seems that Christians misunderstood the loving message of Jesus. Or did they?

If we are to analyze the morality of Christianity today, we have to accept that it is clearly different from the morality of Christianity in the medieval ages and even more so from its morality in the time of Jesus. This morality is nothing close to what Aquinas or Luther thought it was. They would hardly recognize a Protestant living in America. It is debatable whether they would call for his burning at the stake for heresy.

I remember my shock when coming to Canada and witnessing the Christianity here in my late teens compared to the much more serious Christianity of my Slovakian friends back home. I can imagine that the difference between Calvin and ourselves is much more significant. As Kenan Malik writes, "moral codes," whether they are religious or secular, are the result of "social structures and needs."[1] Today many of us vocally desire rights for women, justice against police brutality, and equal treatment. In medieval Christendom, these concerns would not have had any light of day. These distinctions will help narrow the scope of the analysis in this chapter.

In this chapter, I want to primarily make a defense, or "steel-man," the Christian right's morality as it exists today. I will point out the good, the bad, and the ugly. And I will try to be balanced.

The Bible's Commandments in Context

The Bible's commandments have to be understood in the context they are presented in. To agree with the morality of the Christian right, you have to accept a set of premises to contextualize the wrongdoings ordained by God in the Bible. For one, to understand Christian ethics, you have to agree with the message of the Gospel. Secondly, you have to think that humans are crippled by their unreasonableness and cannot understand God's ways (what I discussed in Chapter One, Christianity and an Age of Unreason). And lastly, you must accept that a lot is at stake for Christians, namely eternal damnation or salvation.

Of course, many will reject these basic assumptions, making it difficult to prove that Christian ethics are best for society. If you do not accept Jesus as the real Son of God and the Creator of the Universe, Christian ethics may seem damning, appalling, and even barbaric, as they do for many.

One of Christianity's foremost critics, Richard Dawkins, for example, finds Christian morality particularly devastating to society and accuses God of every negative adjective imaginable in his book, *The God Delusion*. Christians who object to Dawkins forget that any unsaved observer of the Bible has no reason to think the behavior that is condoned in the Bible is morally upright. Christians should not be so offended. When Michael Shermer writes that the Bible is one of the most "immoral works in all of literature," it really should not come as a surprise.[2] Need I remind you that at one point in the Old Testament, God calls for the complete killing of "anything that breathes," which included the Hittites, Amorites, Canaanites, Perizzites, Hibites, and Jebusites (Deuteronomy 20:16)?

Can we suspect that not even one of these men and women were unsuspecting adults minding their own business to the best of their abilities for the time they were living in? Or do we blame them for the immoral behavior of the time? In another revealing moment, God calls for the killing of all the Amalekites, including the "men and women, children and infants, cattle and sheep, camels and donkeys" (1 Samuel 15:2). Any sane person living in the 21st century would condemn the actions of any state committing atrocities like this today. So why not then?

Protests against violence are regular occurrences in today's society because we find them appalling and unjust. When the Christian objects to Dawkins and other critics of Christianity, they need first to recognize what we touched on in the first chapter: the Gospel is foolishness to those who are perishing. As a Christian, you can only reason with your secular friend to an extent — the rest is up to God.

The Gospel, the Foolishness of Unbelievers, & Hell

As I said above, to understand the morality of the Bible, we must understand the Gospel's message. The Gospel is the story that Jesus came to save sinners from eternal damnation by sacrificing His own life so that everyone might have access to eternal

life with God. Thus, the killing and the incessant call for sacrifices in the Old Testament is setting up the stage for the need
of a Savior. Because, if the Savior did not come, we would still
have to sacrifice lambs and other livestock to God for our sins.
Most importantly, faith would not be enough to save; we would
have to be set apart by works. Jesus' sacrifice, however, the sacrifice of the purest of lambs, covers all sin, setting the record
straight between humanity and God.

In the Old Testament, God is not so ready to forgive the
sins of humanity. Apart from the passages that I mentioned
above, God had to punish humanity at one point by flooding the
earth. Presently, He has to punish sinners by sending them to
hell. Yes. God does send people to hell (I will discuss this more in
my chapter eleleven, The Meaning of Life & the Christian).

Sin separates us from God. Sin is the antithesis of God. This
is one of the central components of His character. He is holy.
Christian teachings may seem weird, outdated, maybe cruel,
but for the Christian, this is the reality they live in. Sin is the
path to death. And since Adam and Eve fell, we have been punished along with them. As an atheist, if you are reading this, you
must understand these basic assumptions to understand the
logic behind Christian moral commandments.

Christian Objective Morality

With those premises out of the way, let's look at the morality
of the Christian right. Christian morality, first and foremost, as
Christian apologists claim, is a set of universalizable behavioral
principles. As Paul writes, every person has the law "written on
their hearts" (Romans 2:15). In other words, Christians believe
that our morality is entrenched within us, or hard-wired into
our brains by God.

Along with this, however, God has also revealed commandments in the form of divine command (the Ten Commandments, the Prophets, etc.). It is not only that God's divine revelation reveals commandments, but instead that this morality
is apparent to each one of us without revelation, according to

Paul. There are problems with this assumption, of course, but let us accept it to be able to move on for the time being.

The Christian philosophical assumption is that our comprehension of morality relies on our understanding that both good and evil exist within society. Good and evil are directly related to the existence of a moral law because otherwise, there would be no "objective" or "universalizable" principle to establish morals with. This argument can be seen in the form that Ravi Zacharias presented it in:

> If there's evil, then there's good.
> If there's good, then there's a moral law.
> If there's a moral law, then there must be a moral lawgiver.
> If there's no moral lawgiver, then there's no moral law
> If there's no moral law, then there's no good.
> If there's no good, then there's no evil
> If there's no evil. What was your question?
>
> Why do I have to assume a moral lawgiver? Every time that question is raised it is either raised by a person or about a person. Therefore, its premise is that there is value to the person. But naturalism does not provide value to personhood. [3]

This is usually the way Christian apologists defend objective morality. First, they point out that evil exists and that if evil exists, then good must exist in conjunction with it. Otherwise, it would be impossible to know how to define good, they insist. Then they claim that moral laws must be objective, above society and time; Otherwise, they'd be irrelevant.

The argument for objective morality has been defended to the extent that the Gospel has been preached. Timothy Keller, when discussing objective morality in his book *Making Sense of God*, explained that "If there is no God . . . it creates a great problem in that there doesn't appear to be an alternative moral source that exists outside of our inner feelings and intuitions."[4] Similarly, John C. Lennox writes: "I am not suggesting that science cannot help us to make ethical judgments. For instance, knowing about how much pain animals feel can help shape judgments on animal testing. But the judgment is made on the basis of a prior moral conviction, that pain and misery is a bad thing."[5] In other words, outside sources can help in establishing moral right and wrong, but the moral convictions have to be separate from our intuitions. In the words of Wayne Grudem, "[T]he Bible is our only absolute authority for defining moral right and wrong."[6]

The point all these Christian thinkers are touching on is that there is an ambivalence to justice in naturalism. The solution to that ambivalence is objective universalizable morality that can only be given by God. They claim that we cannot have any morality without a justice that is above this fallen world.

Moral Agreement
Christian apologists further claim that the objective morality presented in the Bible will be able to give us moral agreement amongst each other. Thus, Keller writes:

> Hume, Kant, Kierkegaard, and others sought to provide justification for objective moral claims. But they all failed, and this is why our society today is driven by polarized, irreconcilable, alternate universes of moral discourse, none of which can convince the others in the slightest.[7]

The idea Keller presents is, however, slightly misleading. In fact, it misrepresents the broad agreement that many philosophers have with one another. Yes, moral philosophers will disagree in philosophy classrooms and debates because they usually discuss controversial moral issues. Otherwise, there would be no point in their contributions and discussions. The moral questions that we have largely settled are rarely discussed because they are not philosophically-interesting. As

A. C. Grayling explains, "I would be surprised to find fellow humanists disagreeing very greatly, or about much."[8] There is some utility to Keller's argument, nonetheless. It can show how Christians often believe that secular thinkers are divided because there is no "objectivity" or objective basis for their philosophical arguments concerning morality.

Morality Within Us

Critics of the Christian right's morality might say that if morality is indeed entrenched within us, as the Bible says it is, then that fails to explain why both Christians and atheists behave immorally at times. But the Bible is evident in that it says that we are fallen beings that have strayed from God. Our fallen nature would explain why humans regularly fail to live in line with the moral law within us.

In his latest book, *Outgrowing God*, Dawkins cites a study that says that a convicted criminal is 750 times more likely to be a Christian than an atheist.[9] But Dawkins, along with others, forget that the Bible never claims that Christian teaching will necessarily result in people behaving better. It definitely could. But humans are fallen and regularly act in ways that God condemns. Furthermore, there is a fundamental difference between biblical and non-biblical Christians and their behavior. More importantly, when Dawkins cites this study, he fails to mention the sociological reasons for their crimes, which are relevant. It is hard to imagine that Christians who dwell on God's Word every day and are committed to preaching the Gospel in love will engage in criminal behavior more often than anyone else on average.

In *Beyond Opinion*, Alison Thomas quotes some research that highlights this important distinction between biblical and non-biblical Christians and their behavior. Thomas writes that "committed Christians" are "twice as likely to volunteer time to help the needy," "five times less likely to report that their careers come first," and "nine times more likely to avoid Internet pornography."[10] The criteria that distinguish committed Christians from uncommitted Christians, as outlined by Thomas, are their beliefs in absolute moral truths; that God is all-knowing and all-powerful; that Jesus was without sin; that Satan exists; that salvation is a gift; that every Christian has a duty to spread the Gospel; and that the Bible is without error in its teaching.[11] Thus, Thomas concludes that "orthodoxy matters" concerning the ethical behavior of Christians.[12]

When it comes to orthodoxy, many scholars debate the historical and scriptural importance of some of the passages that I will discuss in this chapter. Debatably, the views of the Christian right are most aligned with that of both historical Christendom and the scholarly exegesis of the Bible. It is unlikely that those who want to stick with the orthodox scriptural texts will fit nicely into society as it progresses.

The solution to this is not clear apart from separating church and state, which I will discuss at more length in Chapter Five (The Human Rights of the Christian). I simply want to outline the more important distinctions in Christian thinking concerning morality for my purposes here. I do recommend consulting further literature on all of these topics as I am nowhere close to doing them justice.

Sexuality

First, I want to discuss the Christian right's view on sexuality. It is important to note that Christians believe that sex between a married couple, as God designed it to be, is "good" (Gen 1:27-28, 31). The language in the Bible that is used for sexual intercourse within the covenant of marriage is one where the two "know" one another (Gen 4:17, 25; 24:16; Num. 31:17; 1 Kings 1:4).[13] So, the biblical understanding is that when two people engage in sexual intercourse, they are deeply intertwined with one another in a meaningful way. Thus, the Bible celebrates sexuality. This can be seen most apparently in the book Song of Solomon in the Bible, a book that reads like an erotic love song or poem to Solomon's lover.

Biblical Christians believe that any sexual activity before marriage is sinful, including sexual thought. In some ways, the Christian commitment toward sexual chastity can be commendable. Since when has self-control been bad? The question, however, is how far is too far and whether self-control can lead to trauma.

When it comes to abstaining from watching pornography, for example, and the health benefits, the research is mixed. Some studies show the benefits of masturbation and pornography. Others say that it causes erectile dysfunction and the mistreatment of women, among other things. The latter is often associated with Christian organizations, so it is difficult to make much of their biases or lack thereof.

One of the leading voices of the *NoFap* community, for example, after leaving the organization, has testified that his erectile dysfunction had much more to do with the moral conflicts he had surrounding sex and anxiety. When he realized this, he stopped blaming porn for his dysfunction.[14] Excessive use of anything can damage your brain, and pornography is definitely among those things. So, abstinence and mediocrity should both be celebrated for those that do not adapt to Christian morality.

Critics will say that the Christian view of sexuality is unlivable. But the underlying premise of Jesus' "Orwellian" call that sexual thoughts of others that are not your spouse are sin, is not that you should be tormented by your sinfulness but rather that you should turn your focus to the Cross. The Cross is the central message of the Gospel. Therefore, the idea of Christian repentance can provide a consolable world. The Christian life is not solely about acting well and biblically. Instead, it is about loving God and loving your neighbor above all else, as Jesus said. Commandments come because of love, and there can be some consolation in that.

Homosexuality or Same-sex Relations

When it comes to same-sex relations, the Bible is, unfortunately, also crystal clear. The Bible teaches that homosexuality is a sin. However, the Bible does not exalt "homosexual sin" over other sins. More importantly, the Bible calls for preaching the truth in love (Ephesians 4:15) and gentleness and respect (1 Peter 3:15). So, when Christians are called to preach the Gospel to those who are attracted to the same sex, they have no right to exalt that sin over other heterosexual sin outside of marriage.

As much as Christians are called to condemn the "sin" of same-sex relations, they are, to an equal extent, called to condemn other sins as well. However, we cannot eliminate the outdated passages that condemn homosexuality in the Bible. The Bible says the following about same-sex relations:

> You shall not lie with a male as one lies with a female; it is an abomination. Also you shall not have intercourse with any animal to be defiled with it, nor shall any woman stand before an animal to mate with it; it is a perversion. Do not defile yourselves by any of these things; for by all these the nations which I am casting out before you have become defiled. Leviticus 18:22-24

> If there is a man who lies with a male as those who lie with a woman, both of them have committed a detestable act; they shall surely be put to death. Their bloodguiltiness is upon them. Leviticus 20:13

> In the same way the men also abandoned natural relations with women and were inflamed with lust for one another. Men committed shameful acts with other men, and received in themselves the due penalty for their error. Romans 1:27

> We also know that the law is made not for the righteous but for lawbreakers and rebels, the ungodly and sinful, the unholy and irreligious, for those who kill their fathers or mothers, for murderers, for the sexually immoral, for those practicing homosexuality, for slave traders and liars and perjurers—and for

whatever else is contrary to the sound doctrine that conforms to the gospel concerning the glory of the blessed God, which he entrusted to me. 1 Timothy 1:9-11

Don't you know that the unrighteous will not inherit God's kingdom? Do not be deceived: No sexually immoral people, idolaters, adulterers, or anyone practicing homosexuality, no thieves, greedy people, drunkards, verbally abusive people, or swindlers will inherit God's kingdom. 1 Corinthians 6:9-10

But why are same-sex relations frowned upon in the Bible? John MacArthur, one of the leading voices of the Christian right in the United States, in a sermon on Romans 1 concerning homosexuality, argues that it is because homosexuality is among the things that "God hates" and that it "brings God's judgment."[15] Biblically, he is right; God brought judgment on Sodom and Gomorrah because of their homosexual practices, among other things (Gen. 19:1-28, note: v.5; Jude 7). MacArthur goes so far to say that same-sex marriage is an "oxymoron" since it's "impossible."[16]

Timothy Keller makes a more descriptive point on why God outlawed same-sex practices in the Bible. In a talk at *Google*, he says: "The Christian view of marriage says it's between a man and a woman because the genders mesh and clash," bringing these two genders together to "change each other in ways that we wouldn't otherwise."[17] However, he makes sure to say that this is the Christian view, which he thinks will arguably not prevail in culture.

Christians should take note of Keller on how to talk about their moral differences with society. I think it is an absolute waste of time for the Christian to persuade non-Christians to behave the way that the Bible urges. Sinners will not become believers by behaving in a way that the Bible condones. Should we similarly also make premarital sex illegal? Because it would not be surprising if the latter was harming society more than the former because of its much larger prevalence among the youth. Although, that is not clear at all as well.

The Christian right prioritizes several other ethical issues. In the West, the Christian right has been on the forefront of our culture wars, from abortion to same-sex marriage to free speech to liberty, and so forth. And it is understandable why they would focus on these issues. We will look at these specifically when we discuss the human rights of the Christian in Chapter Five. For now, I want to turn to some of the positive aspects in Christian ethics.

Positive Side-Effects

As I hope to have shown, some of these strict moral codes are useful guidelines that help keep society in check. The beatitudes in Jesus' sermon on the mount (a call for the poverty of spirit, meekness, mournfulness, righteousness, mercifulness, purity of heart, peaceableness, and persecution for righteousness) are admirable calls (Mat 5-7). Christian communities are called to exhibit love, gentleness, and respect, rather than harsh judgment and victimization. The Bible also calls not to judge others (Luke 6:37), tell the truth (Col 3:9), be merciful (Luke 6:36), forgive (Mat 6:14-15), witness to unbelievers (1 Peter 2:12), strive to live in peace with others (Hebrews 12:14), give to others (Prov 21:26), and so forth. Jesus says that Christians should "love one another" as He loved them (John 15:12; John 13:34-35). Above all, everything that Christians do must be done in love (1 Cor 16:14).

In an infamous passage on the Christian love that Christians should have for one another, Paul writes:

> Love is patient and kind; love does not envy or boast; it is not arrogant or rude. It does not insist on its own way; it is not irritable or resentful; it does not rejoice at wrongdoing, but rejoices with the truth. Love bears all things, believes all things, hopes all things, endures

all things. 1 Cor 13:4-7

This passage, because it has been repeated at weddings *ad infinitum*, has made people think Paul is discussing romantic love, when in fact he is discussing Christian love. For the Christian, the love that Christ calls for from his disciples is boundless; It extends to your neighbor (Rom 13:8-10); the unworthy (Luke 5:31-32); and your enemies (Luke 6:32-36).

In *The Evolution of God*, Robert Wright argues that passages such as the ones mentioned above helped the early Church stay together. The commandments to remain pure and abide by the rules allowed the Church to prevent any large squabbles. Wright continues,

> [I]f you're going to start a religion that becomes the most powerful recruiting machine in the history of the world, an appealing message is only half the battle. The message has to not just attract people, but get them to behave in ways that sustain the religious organization and spread it.[18]

Thus, when Paul calls for the Galatians to avoid sins he makes sure to make the list long, including "fornication, impurity, licentiousness, idolatry, sorcery, enmities, strife, jealousy, anger, quarrels, dissensions, factions, envy, drunkenness, carousing, and things like these."[19] Wright explains that most of these sins that Paul lists cause divisions within communities, like envy, anger, jealousy, and strife. Therefore, by restricting and excommunicating members who behave in this way, early Christians prevented major divisions among them. Christians today then have a nicely put together system of moral codes to choose from to avoid needless bickering.

Negative Side-Effects
Along with the positives come the negatives. Christian morality also stresses what could be thought of as an unhealthy amount of holiness in the lives of believers. In Isaiah, God is de-

scribed as "Holy, Holy, Holy," (Isaiah 6:3) and God expects his Church to resemble Him in that holiness (1 Peter 1:16).

Some estimates suggest that there are more than 1,000 commandments in the New Testament alone. That number is mostly irrelevant, however. Any reader of the Bible will notice the theme that God expects specific behavior of His people. In the end, there is a holiness without which Christians will not see God (Hebrew 12:14). It is not only that Christians are atoned once and for all and can act in any way they desire; Jesus expects His people to actually follow His commandments.

I would be remiss not to mention that some of these doctrines concerning sexuality will harm Christians. I do intuitively believe that the negatives concerning the Christian right's view on sexuality can outweigh the positives when it comes to society. Still, it is worth noting that the positives are possible. As I said before, self-control is admirable, but too much may lead to trauma and guilt. For example, historically, Christianity (and other religions) have celebrated virginity and ostracized soon-to-be-wed non-virgins. And it is hard to see why this doctrine was necessary or good for society. In today's world, these shackles should be abandoned along with their cruel judgments.

Similarly, when it comes to the more complex issue of gender non-binary individuals, or "transgender individuals" (a term that is not used as often anymore but people recognize more), one that is above this short chapter on Christian morality, Christians also make harmful comments.

The Christian right specifically will often claim that God created two sexes: men and women. They then selectively hand-pick research that suggests that children are better off raised if they are told what sex they are from an early age or with parents of both sexes rather than parents in same-sex marriages.[20] Society is rapidly progressing and is in need of providing more rights to its citizens and the Christian right is still adamantly arguing against doing so.

Christians should be reminded that their morality does

not have to be culture's morality, as Keller argued. And that indeed, they can act differently if society chooses the more progressive route. We do not have to agree; Our moral biases and convictions will often not let us agree.

The Old vs. New Testament Morality

There is also the question whether there is a substantial difference between the morality of the Old and New Testament. Many Christians in the 21st century may have abandoned what they think of as an "archaic" understanding of God from the Old Testament. Some modern-day Christians call the troubling passages that condone violence or the blatantly unscientific ones in the Old Testament, allegorical. Others disagree.

MacArthur claims that he is a Christian because of the Old Testament.[21] He explains that without the Old Testament, he would not see the evidence for Jesus being the Messiah. Indeed, biblically, it is challenging to get rid of the Old Testament. If you were to do so, you would be arguing directly against the teaching of Jesus.

To remind you, Jesus said that "I and the Father are one" (John 10:30), "The father is in me and I in the father" (John 14:11), and "Whoever has seen me has seen the Father" (John 14:9). In other passages, Jesus claims that "it is easier for heaven and earth" to vanish than for "a stroke of pen to drop out of the Law" (Luke 16:17; also Matthew 5:17). Christians have to accept the Old Testament; Otherwise, they would be arguing in direct juxtaposition with the teachings of Jesus.

The rest of society is not so quick to accept the morality of the Old Testament. In fact, when the conservative commentator and radio host, Dr. Laura Schlessinger, cited the Old Testament as the basis for denouncing same-sex partnership (Lev 18:22), she unsurprisingly received a fair share of criticism, including a sarcastic letter testifying to the backward logic of using a verse from the Old Testament to justify behavior today. The letter read,

Dear Dr. Laura,

Thank you for doing so much to educate people regarding God's Law. I have learned a great deal from your show, and I try to share that knowledge with as many people as I can. When someone tries to defend the homosexual lifestyle, for example, I simply remind him that Leviticus 18:22 clearly states it to be an abomination. End of debate.

I do need some advice from you, however, regarding some of the specific laws and how to best follow them.

When I burn a bull on the altar as a sacrifice, I know it creates a pleasing odour for the Lord (Lev. 1:9). The problem is my neighbors. They claim the odour is not pleasing to them. Should I smite them?

I would like to sell my daughter into slavery, as sanctioned in Exodus 21:7. In this day and age, what do you think would be a fair price for her?

I know that I am allowed no contact with a woman while she is in her period of menstrual uncleanliness (Lev. 15:19-24). The problem is, how do I tell her? I have tried asking, but most women take offense.

Lev. 25:44 states that I may indeed possess slaves, both male and female, provided they are purchased from neighboring nations. A friend of mine claims that this applies to Mexicans, but not Canadians. Can you clarify? Why can't I own Canadians?

I have a neighbor who insists on working on the Sabbath. Exodus 35:2 clearly states he should be put to death. Am I morally obligated to kill him myself?...
Your devoted disciple and adoring fan,
J. Kent Ashcraft.[22]

The sarcastic tone will stop some from taking the logic seriously. But it is worth pointing out that defending the view that same-sex relations are sinful to unbelievers by using the Old Testament is mostly futile and comes across as selective. In the end, unbelievers reject your God's existence so why coerce their behavior by following the Bible's morals? That is not to say that biblical Christians do not have a responsibility to preach God's moral standards. Instead, Christians should not expect unbelievers to follow these moral standards for their own sake necessarily. Grudem argues that only through the "work of the Spirit of God" will sinners recognize that "the words of Scripture are, in fact, the words of God."[23] Biblically, that is correct teaching, and others should act accordingly.

I do not deny that the Bible is, at times, morally revealing or insightful. All I am saying here is that God is undoubtedly above morality as we understand it in the 21st century. To see eye to eye, we must first agree that we can differ on moral issues. It is okay to disagree with one another. Disagreement is necessary.

We have seen that in order to understand Christian ethics, which often can seem outdated, you first have to accept two premises: (1) the message of Christianity (the Gospel), (2) that humans are crippled by their unreasonableness. It is in light of these two premises that Christians think about ethics. Ideally, they differentiate between cultural ethics and Christian ethics, meaning that they would not enforce their standards on society. In the end, it is undoubtedly necessary for us to agree to disagree, so to speak, if we are to have flourishing democracies.

Chapter 4

Atheism & Moral Insight

[T]he Bible is one long celebration of violence. – Steven Pinker[1]

[T]he teaching of Christ as it appears in the Gospels, has had extraordinarily little to do with the ethics of Christians. The most important thing about Christianity, from a social and historical point of view, is not Christ but the church. – Bertrand Russell[2]

Society is increasingly polarized over our conflicting moral biases, whether on abortion, same-sex relations, premarital sex, lying, or religion. We touched on some of these issues in the previous chapter. I can expect that many of you disagreed with some of the assumptions and positions of the Christian right and even Christians more broadly since many within Christianity subscribe to socially conservative views.

To reiterate, for the Christian, our moral positions are intuitive (our moral compass) or given to us by divine revelation (divine command). For the atheist, our moral positions are at times intuitive, but also intellectually derived, rather than given to us by God. In other words, our moral convictions are defended despite our natural intuition and acted on despite a natural inclination to do otherwise.

There are many things Christians and atheists agree upon, however, despite having different reasons for doing so. For example, few alive today would say that it is okay to kill someone who sleeps with your wife or even that it is okay to chop off a kid's hand if they steal from you.

The question of what constitutes the best moral action has been debated for millennia from the time of the Ancient Greek and Eastern philosophers to the tweeting of Trump. 2,000 years ago, Plato, along with Aristotle, thought that a virtuous and moral man was one who abstained from 'the passions,' which included the various sensations we feel when we experience pleasure and instead directed their focus to the life of 'the mind.' Epicurus partly disagreed with them and believed that experiencing bodily sensations was necessary and moral. David Hume, famously posited that it is impossible to justify moral actions since we cannot obtain absolute proof for having them without appealing to a metaphysical deity. Instead, Hume believed that morality was a social contract between citizens to maintain order in society. Jeremy Bentham claimed that morality was entirely dependent on consequences. For Bentham, the best moral catalyst was 'the greatest amount of happiness for the greatest number of people.' Since then, many others have posited fascinating thought experiments to prove that categorizing moral actions based on consequences is not enough.

Today, we take moral reasoning particularly seriously because of the development of Artificial Intelligence (AI). The author, Yuval Noah Harari, even speculates that one of the last jobs that will be automated in the 21st century is that of a philosopher because they will have to work closely with engineers who program the behavior of AI.[3]

Together we ask, what if we programmed consequentialist reasoning into AI? Is it ever justifiable to infringe on someone's freedom to guarantee equality to the collective? Moral philosophers have stumbled onto many difficult questions that are seemingly impossible to resolve since they've been disputed for centuries. But these questions are increasingly relevant with the development of surveillance technology and potentially autonomous AI, or Artificial Super Intelligence, as some like to call it. We do not have the answer to what the best moral actions are; We can debate endlessly.

Morality and Who is Most Moral?

As we have seen from the previous chapter, Christians hold that moral laws are universal and given to us either by divine revelation (the Ten Commandments, Beatitudes, etc.) or are within us (our moral compass or conscience). Along with having a soul, Christians believe that this is what distinguishes us from animals. However, morality can be understood more broadly and does not have to depend on revelation. This is where atheists and Christians disagree.

But what is morality in the first place? In the previous chapter, I defined Chrisitan morality as a "set of universalizable behavioral principles." Let me elaborate since there is no simple way to define morality. Robert Solomon wrote in his widely read textbook *Introducing Philosophy*, "Morality is a set of fundamental rules that guide our actions."[4] According to Harvard psychologist Joshua Greene, morality is a "set of psychological adaptations that allow otherwise selfish individuals to reap the benefits of social co-operation."[5] Michael Shermer writes that "Morality involves how we think and act toward other moral agents in terms of whether our thoughts and actions are right or wrong concerning their survival and flourishing."[6]

Nowhere in these definitions do we have the proposition that these "adaptations" or "rules" are universal. Although some atheists argue that, similar to Christians, morality can be universalized. This argument was most notably promoted by one of the most known moral philosophers of the 20th century, John Rawls. This attempt has been met with a fair share of hostility, however. In response to Rawls' universal morality, Mark Johnson writes:

> I will suggest it is morally irresponsible to think and
> act as though we possess a universal, disembodied

reason that generates absolute rules, decision-making procedures, and universal or categorical laws by which we can tell right from wrong in any situation we encounter.[7]

Many disagree with the premise that universal morality is crucial and somehow binding. The question is, why do we even need universal morality? Why do Christians think that universals justify morality in the first place?

Universality

Christian apologists argue that by abandoning "Judeo-Christian values," our culture will inevitably lead to anarchy and nihilism. Indeed, this seems to be a commonly held view by most Christian apologists. Timothy Keller argues that by rejecting divine revelation for moral truths, Enlightenment thinkers disposed of "a *telos* for human beings," implying that any reason for behaving morally was lost with the Enlightenment.[8] Similarly, in his book *Gunning for God*, John C. Lennox argues that "[A]theism does not supply any intellectual foundation for morality."[9] According to the geneticist and evangelical, Francis Collins, "[I]f the moral law is just a side effect of evolution, then there is no such thing as good and evil."[10]

Christian apologists believe that to have objective morality, moral truths have to have been eternal; they could not have been the mere happenstance of evolution because that would suggest that our morals were random and arbitrary. Putting theory aside, studies reveal that everyday people behave morally without having any objective basis for morality. For some reason, atheists still think it worthwhile to treat their neighbors decently.

Atheists and Decency

It is not that difficult to see whether these Christian apologists are correct in their arguments since their evidence has to be empirical. In one sense, their propositions are too simple to be true. If only God grants universal morality, and there is no basis for behaving well, then we should be able to see that directly reflected in society. Unsurprisingly, many have devoted decades of research into this question.

For instance, Gregory S. Paul compared the moral behavior of seventeen economically developed nations in his *Journal of Religion and Society* (2005) and concluded that "higher rates of belief in and worship of a creator correlate with higher rates of homicide, juvenile and early mortality, STD infection rates, teen pregnancy and abortion in the prosperous democracies."[11] These findings may just explain a correlation rather than the cause as we saw from the previous chapter. Economically developed nations have better education systems, prosperity, job opportunities, and criminal systems, lessening the likelihood of criminal behavior.

Since people behave well without teaching Christian morality, what is the point in teaching it in the first place? Or, as Shermer points out in his comments concerning Paul's findings, "[I]f religion is such a powerful force for societal health, then why is America – the most religious nation in the Western world – also the unhealthiest on all of these social measures?"[12] It is not as simple as saying that Christians will always behave better than atheists. That is simply not true. Perhaps, biblical Christians behave better than average atheists (rather than mindful humanists), as I argued in the previous chapter. If we do not compare two sets of similarly mindful people on opposing ideological spectrums, we are comparing apples and oranges.

Although, Phil Zukerman observed that societies with the lowest rates of belief in a god are more prosperous, free, equal, democratic, conscious of women's rights, human rights, have a higher life expectancy, lower crime rates, and higher educational attainment (with the exceptions of China, Vietnam, and Russia). These include Sweden, Denmark, the Czech Republic, Japan, Canada, Norway, Finland, China, New Zealand, South Korea, Estonia, France, the Netherlands, Slovenia, Germany, Hungary, Great Britain, Australia, and Belgium.[13] In the United States, among the most Christian nations on Earth, of the twenty-five states with the lowest crime rate, approximately 62 percent are Democratic majority, 38 percent are Republican majority. Similarly:

> Of the twenty-five most dangerous cities, 76 percent are in red states, and 24 percent are in blue states. In fact, three of the five most dangerous cities in the U.S. are in the pious state of Texas. The twelve states with the highest rates of burglary are red. Twenty-four of the twenty-nine states with the highest rates of theft are red. Of the twenty-two states with the highest rates of murder, seventeen are red.[14]

Christianity is not the only belief system that can sustain some good behavior in society. Otherwise, these trends would be non-existent. However, most Christians will not disagree with that sentiment because they believe that God put a moral conscience, or moral compass, within each one of us. Christians, as D. Stephen Long writes, "agree that all humans are capable of ethical action."[15] This belief goes back as far as Pierre Bayle (1647-1706 CE), who claimed that atheists could, in fact, have ethical societies and to Baruch Spinoza (1632-1677 CE).

Our Faulty Moral Compass

The belief that we all have a moral compass raises other questions: Why did the Nazis not have that moral compass? Or, Why was torture and capital punishment so prevalent in the medieval ages and beyond? If this moral compass was implanted within us, as the Christians claim, we would be able to reliably see that not only Christians behave differently throughout history but that each one of us does – universally and consistently.

With regard to Christian behavior, we could, in response, argue that once again, very few Christians in the past had redeeming faith that changes behavior. Then, of course, we would dismiss the notion that there is a moral compass and come back to the reality of Christian teaching that only regenerated Christians behave differently from the rest of society. So, then, where is this "objective morality" that God has bestowed upon us? It's not with the people of the past. It seems like the "moral compass" within us is the product of society. In other words, it is outside and not within.

Of course, each one of these questions could have volumes written in response to them. For now, I want to push those who have not thought about these questions. It is not as easy as Collins, Lennox, Keller, and other Christian apologists would suggest.

Do Atheists Have Good Reasons to be Moral?

In the end, when all laws and punishments are taken from us, what prevents atheists from stealing, cheating, and raping? Yes, our behavior results from societal influence, but atheists also have another very compelling reason to behave morally: genes – the ultimate moral compass. For the Christian, evolution is not a satisfactory answer because that would suggest that morality evolved by accident, as we have seen above. Keller writes that evolutionary reasons for morality come across as a "trick that our biology or society has played on us."[16] He says that even if loving altruistic behavior helped our ancestors survive, it doesn't necessarily invoke a moral obligation for us today.

How our ancestors survived, of course, does shape our behavior. Much of our understanding of human behavior rests on this basic premise. When someone is on a diet and cannot stop eating chocolate, nutritious experts explain that this "irrational behavior" is a misguided function of evolution. When studies show that repeated walks outside improve productivity, psychologists explain that it is because of the habitat of our ancestors – where our genes come from.[17] When we help a friend in need, and they help us in return, this encourages good behavior, which encourages genes that enforce this behavior to be passed down. Indeed, we can say with some degree of certainty that genes influence human behavior as much as our environment does.[18]

In his book, *The God Delusion*, Richard Dawkins elaborates

on why genes pass down good behavior. He writes that it is not uncommon for genes to "ensure their selfish survival by influencing organisms to behave altruistically."[19] Dawkins then lists four different Darwinian explanations for why individuals were altruistic or 'moral' to one another:

1. Genetic kinship.
2. Reciprocation: the repayment of favors given and the anticipating of favors given back.
3. The Darwinian benefit of acquiring a reputation for generosity and kindness.
4. (Theory) Conspicuous generosity (Altruistic giving may be an advertisement of dominance or superiority).[20]

Dawkins writes that altruism would be promoted in early human beings for any one of these reasons.[21] Natural selection programmed our brains to have altruistic and sexual urges, hunger, and even xenophobic tendencies. So, Dawkins writes, when a woman is on the pill, and her partner and herself still feel the urge to procreate, that desire is "independent of the ultimate Darwinian pressure that drove it."[22] And the same applies to altruism: "In ancestral times, we had the opportunity to be altruistic only towards close kin and potential reciprocators.... Nowadays that restriction is no longer there, but the rule ... persists.... It is just like sexual desire."[23]

Robert Boyd and Peter Richerson have argued that for humans, cooperation beyond kin and tribal members had started occurring after agriculture had developed, about 10,000 years ago. When food was scarce, tribes competed, forcing tribes to alienate themselves from one another, except when it came to annual gatherings where tribes came to access tools and goods.[24] As communities started growing, there were more advantages to trading, and for tribes to interact and cooperate to gain an advantage over other tribes.[25]

Altruism Across the Animal Kingdom

Importantly, cooperation is not unique to humans, which makes the case for evolutionary morality even stronger. If humans are unique in their moral capacity, then maybe we could argue that God implanted a moral compass within us even if our sinful desires often take over that compass. And, of course, Christians do not necessarily have to be against evolution. They could say that God used evolution to implant the moral compass within us. However, because of the observed universality of altruism across most species, this explanation is not so compelling.

That is primarily because elephants and whales, who have evolved independently from us, have similar tendencies for friendship and social lives.[26] Indeed, Nicholas Christakis writes that the observable independently-evolved morality of elephants and whales "demonstrates that this pattern of traits – the social suite – is adaptive and coherent."[27] We would then have to argue that God gave most species a moral compass. That is possible, but we have no reason to accept it.

The morality of non-human animals is a fascinating field of study. Patricia S. Churchland writes of numerous instances of interspecies cooperation. She writes of ravens leading coyotes to an elk carcass, humans and dogs cooperating for as long as 30,000 years, baboons used by humans to help guide stray goats, and so forth. Different species help one another and understand each other's needs.

In one instance, Churchland recounts of a story where the female baboon Ahla, "led the farmer's goats out in the morning, gave alarm calls if she spotted a predator, brought the goats back to the barn in the evening, groomed the goats, and regularly escorted separated juvenile goats back to their mothers."[28] Indeed, animals born with rare mutations that make them indifferent to their environments are less likely to survive and procreate.[29] Thus, it makes sense that we can observe altruistic behavior in the animal kingdom since it helps survival.

Many will read this and the fact that we act morally because of evolutionary reasons as a precursor to abandoning morality altogether. Keller writes, "[W]hat has been generally beneficial to the species over the ages may not be particularly beneficial to an individual in the present," and "if morality is really a matter of benefit rather than of spiritual obligation transcending personal concerns," then any set of ethical guidelines "can, like any other useful instrument, be taken up or laid down as one chooses."[30] Because of this, many, along with Keller, conclude that "There's simply no way to tell right from wrong" and that we "shouldn't try."[31]

However, Keller makes one fundamental mistake; Morality is not an instrument, but rather a behavioral obligation that transcends personal willingness to do otherwise. For many, stealing is not a viable way to live even if the option presents itself. Churchland explains that the primary hypothesis on offer for having social values is the "neurochemistry of attachment and bonding in mammals."[32] These are not mere instruments that we can choose to abandon to our liking. We are caring largely because it feels good; Indeed, caring, according to Churchland, is "pretty much all there is."[33] Mammals need care for survival. Piglets, calves, puppies, and humans who do not bond with their mothers cannot survive long.[34] It is not merely, as Keller proposes, a matter of picking up instruments; Instead, our morality is a matter of survival.

More importantly, if we admit that evolutionary reasons are not sufficient in providing a moral law and hence cannot oblige fellow citizens to fulfill basic moral obligations, we still do not get rid of moral obligation, since the consequences to actions still matter, despite them evolving by chance. Even if morality is as Joseph Heath argues, "a complex cultural artifact" and not something that is within our "hearts or our heads," we still do not dispose of our obligation to one another.[35] In reality, whether or not we have an objective basis for behaving morally grounded in divine command, evolution, or because of social cohesion, bears no weight on the state of the world.

It is not clear to me why having an objective metaphysical morality matters in the first place. Because if we come back from our lecture rooms and ivory towers into the real world, we see people behaving morally without ever knowing what divine command, consequentialism, kin altruism, deontology, or any other ethical theories or explanations, are.

Secular - Humanist - Morality

So, what is this secular or "humanist" morality? As I argued before, Socrates, Plato, Aristotle, the Stoics, and Epicureans all debated morality hundreds of years before Jesus even appeared on the scene. That is not to mention the Eastern schools of thought of the Confucianists, Taoists, and Buddhists. Humanism, Grayling writes, is "older by nearly a millennium than Christianity … and as alive now as it was in its origins."[36]

Christians often borrowed from Greek thinkers; Hence, they cannot be seen as a separate ideological entity that produced moral insight out of nowhere. Should we disregard Aristotle's *Nicomachean Ethics*, Marcus Aurelius' *Meditations*, or Jeremy Bentham's utilitarianism simply because they are not Christian, or "objective"? Churchland rightly argues that the morality of these thinkers "is entirely real, and to dismiss it as illusory because they do not share a metaphysics of divine beings borders on the delusional" and that "Such self-certainty is itself morally questionable."[37]

To say that secular individuals are more likely to act selfishly because they do not have God's moral commandments to follow and eternal consequences to their actions is both untrue and simplistic. In the words of Sam Harris:

> While each of us is selfish, we are not merely so. Our own happiness requires that we extend the circle of our self-interest to others—to family, friends, and even to perfect strangers whose pleasures and pains matter to us.[38]

There are plenty of non-selfish secular societies popping up worldwide that think it very much worthwhile to behave altruistically. Greg M. Epstein tells us of the humanist community at Harvard that participates in the worldwide movement *Voluntary Simplicity* (VS). This movement stresses a minimalist lifestyle, all the while recognizing that there are certain things that we can not go without in this world, such as shopping, driving, leisure time, and other essential expenses like personal hygiene. The movement recognizes that there are very few things that we need to make us truly happy. Members of the VS movement are deliberate and conscious about transportation, the environment, recycling, diets, consumption, and also about interacting in a humane manner that is based on "co-operation" and "mutual entertainment."[39]

The VS community is not alone in its mindful lifestyle. Most known among academics is perhaps the philanthropic movement "Effective Altruism" formed by Princeton University professor of bioethics, Peter Singer, and the Oxford University moral philosophers, William MacAskill and Toby Ord. Effective Altruists are concerned with the less fortunate in third world countries, making significant sacrifices to their own lives to have the financial means to contribute to organizations that help those that need it most. MacAskill explains the fundamentals of Effective Altruism in his book *Doing Good Better*:

> [T]he key questions to help you think like an effective altruist: How many people benefit, and by how much? Is this the most effective thing you can do? Is this area neglected? What would have happened otherwise? What are the chances of success, and how good would success be?[40]

Effective altruists donate to non-profit charities such as *80,000 hours, GiveDirectly, Innovations for Poverty Action*, and *GiveWell* that specialize in efficiently using their resources to maximize good. They consider taking career paths that allow them to donate more and have time to focus further on humanitarian causes. They also regularly donate "blood, stem cells, bone marrows, or a kidney to a stranger."[41]

The *Bill & Melinda Gates Foundation, Oxfam,* and other strictly secular organizations have perhaps been the most known contributors to reducing abject poverty. It is because of organizations like these that, as of 2010, one is more likely to die of obesity than starvation in the world.[42]

The Morality of the Christian

Apart from the historical argument that Christians did not behave much better than others; We also have the more pressing matter that the Bible is not a particularly insightful book when it comes to moral behavior. Because of this, my attempt to "steel-man" the Christian position toward morality in the previous chapter was rather difficult.

The biblical scholar Raymund Schwager writes that the Torah, the Hebrew Bible, "contains over six hundred passages" on the killing and destruction of one another.[43] In fact, of these six hundred passages, in more than one hundred, "Yahweh expressly gives the command to kill people."[44] The atrocitologist, Matthew White, estimates that there are about 1.2 million deaths accounted for in the Bible, excluding the half-million deaths between Judah and Israel documented in 2 Chronicles 13 because of the historical impossibility of it ever happening.[45] Noah's Flood would add another 20 million, or so, to that count.[46]

Thus, even if we would grant the historical accuracy of these on-slaughts and massacres, we would have to then account for why God was so blood-thirsty in the first place in the Old Testament and whether there was not another, perhaps, more diplomatic way of cohabitating with neighboring tribes. Of course, Christians can object that God's behavior in the Old Testament testifies to His relationship to sin. In that case, it is hard to disagree; Who are we to understand God (Romans 9:20)? But that certainly does not give enough grounds for accepting the Christian position.

In one memorable passage in the Old Testament, Samson, in what Steven Pinker calls a "9/11-like suicide attack," takes down a building that kills three thousand worshipping men and women.[47] In another passage, Nadab and Abihu, Aaron's eldest two sons, offer a sacrifice to God with a foreign or "unauthorized" fire, disobeying God's instructions, forcing God to consume them in fire (Lev 10:1-3).

In another moment in what seems to be a cosmic game between Satan and God, Satan tests Job's commitment to God, with God's permission, of course, by taking away his wealth, physical health, and killing his children. Job passes God's test, or rather, Satan's test, and gives him more sons and daughters. Even if God granted the killed children a more than pleasant life in the afterlife, it seems like a fiercely unpleasant test, one that many would rightly object to and disregards the autonomy of the individual, that prized Western concept.

The Bible has several other commandments that are contrary to what we think is morally acceptable today, yet we believe they are warranted because God is "above the law." As John M. Frame writes in his book, *Nature's Case For God*, "Everything God does expresses his might, and all his mighty acts are things he has the right to do."[48] Biblically, of course, Frame is correct. God is above the law. Maybe we are above God's law as well then, since we find these passages morally repulsive. If not, what do we do with passages in the Bible that condone evil, genocide, and injustice? These are not stand-alone instances. Here are a few from the Old Testament:

> Now kill all the boys. And kill every woman who has slept with a man, but save for yourselves every girl who has never slept with a man. Numbers 31:17-18

> I am the Lord, and there is none else. I form the light, and create darkness: I make peace, and create evil: I the Lord do all these things. Isaiah 45:7

Therefore, thus says the Lord, Behold, I am bringing evil upon them which they cannot escape though they cry to me, I will not listen to them. Jeremiah 11:11

He [God] destroyeth the perfect and the wicked. If the scourge slays suddenly, he will laugh at the trial of the innocent. The earth is gen into the hand of the wicked; he covereth the faces of the judges thereof; if not, where, and who is he? Job 9:22-24

How oft is the candle of the wicked put out! And how oft cometh their destruction upon them! God distributeth sorrows in his anger. They are as stubble before the wind, and as chaff that the storm carrieth away. God layeth up his iniquity for his children: he rewardeth him, and he shall know it. His eyes shall see his destruction, and he shall drink of the wrath of the Almighty. Job 21:17-20

For thus says the Lord of hosts: 'As I purposed to do evil to you when your father provoked me to wrath, and I did not relent, says the Lord of hosts.' Zechariah 8:14

Thus saith the Lord, Behold, I will bring evil upon this place, and upon the inhabitants thereof, even all the curses that are written in the book which they have read before the king of Judah: Because they have forsaken me, and have burned incense unto other gods. 2 Chronicles 34:24-25

But God sent an evil spirit between Abimelech and the lord of Shechem, and the lords of Shechem dealt treacherously with Abimelech. This happened so that the violence done to the seventy sons of Jerubbaal might be avenged and their blood be laid on their brother Abimelech. Judges 9:23-24

Shall a trumpet be blown in the city, and the people not be afraid? Shall there be evil in a city, and the Lord hath not done it? Amos 3:6

The Lord hath made all things for himself; yea, even the wicked for the day of evil. Proverbs 16:4

Dan Barker in his book, *Mere Morality*, discusses some of these passages and lists the consequences of not listening to God's will, which include "pestilence, consumption, fever, inflammation, fiery heat and drought, blight and mildew, military defeat, death ('Your corpses shall be food for every bird of the air and animal of the earth'), boils, ulcers, scurvy, itch ('of which you cannot be healed'), madness, blindness, confusion of mind, abuse, theft of your property, rape of your wife, business failure, abduction of your children, invasion by rapacious foreigners, servitude, humiliation, unproductive crops."[49] If you do not trust Barker, heed to the Word of God yourself:

If you do not diligently observe all the words of this law that are written in this book, fearing this glorious and awesome name, the Lord your God, then the Lord will overwhelm both you and your offspring with severe and lasting afflictions and grievous and lasting maladies. Deuteronomy 28:58-9

Every other malady and affliction, even though not recorded in the book of this law, the Lord will inflict on you until you are destroyed. Deuteronomy 28:61

You will eat the fruit of your womb, the flesh of your own sons and daughters whom the Lord your God has given you. . . . begrudging even the afterbirth that comes out from between her thighs and the children that she bears, because she is eating them in secret for lack of anything else, in the desperate straits to which

the enemy siege will reduce you in your towns. Deuteronomy 28:53-57

I don't know if the eating of your children is an acceptable punishment under any political system. I firmly believe
that it is unjustifiable even if God has issued a command for
it. What punishment is justifiable? What about when God decided to wipe out the majority of Earth's population, including
all women, children, and innocent animals that cannot freely
choose to sin (Noah's flood)? Is that a justifiable punishment? In
many ways, these commands rest on a logical fallacy, the *argu-
mentum ad baculum*, or "threat of force." And as Grayling rightfully explains, "[P]romises and threats are not a logical justification for acting one way rather than another."[50]

In response, Christians say that these commandments are
historical and culturally specific. They suggest that God's covenant changed and that New Testament morality is much nicer
than Old Testament morality. However, that seems to be contrary to what Jesus says, namely that he did not come to abolish
the Law and the Prophets (Mat 5:17). I touched on that in the
previous chapter.

Even if we reject the Prophets and the Law, Grayling explains that this still does not explain how poor the moral
compass of the New Testament is. In his words, this Christian
"attitude" toward the New Testament is "an odd mixture of lit-
eralism and selective blindness."[51] Grayling elaborates:

> In a few respects, [Christian morality] is the same as
> all other moral systems, in enjoining brotherly love
> and charity: that is a commonplace of any reflection
> on what would make for good lives and societies. But
> then it differs, with its own particular set of injunc-
> tions: give away all your possessions, take no thought
> for tomorrow (consider the lilies of the field), do not
> resist anyone or anything evil (turn the other cheek),
> obey the authorities (render unto Caesar), turn your

back on your family if they disagree with you, do not marry unless you cannot contain yourself sexually. This is the morality of people who genuinely believed that next week or next month the world was to end, that this world does not matter – indeed, is ripe for the furnace – and that one should ignore its demands and realities. This is not a liveable morality.[52]

It certainly seems to be that way. When it comes to the Old Testament and the problematic passages we touched on earlier, some Christians have, believe it or not, sought to defend them. One notable example is the influential Christian apologist William Lane Craig. He writes:

God is not bound by the same moral duties that we are. Our moral duties are established by God's commandments to us . . . but God himself doesn't issue commands to himself, so he doesn't stand under the same moral duties that we do . . . When God commands the Israelites to exterminate the Canaanite clans, they are acting as God's moral agents under his command. So I think that God had the right to command them to do something which, in the absence of a divine command, would have been wrong, but given a divine command, it is not wrong. In fact, it becomes their moral duty.[53]

This explanation can work if you accept that God is real in the first place. But for obvious reasons, many reject that premise and hence cannot find the morality found in the Old Testament, or the New Testament, a coherent moral philosophy. As we have seen, our social environments and our genes act as sufficient explanations. In the end, the universal morality that Christians have for millennia argued is essential in maintaining stability in society is not as necessary as they insist it is. Our laws are debated, and our customs change. History testifies to the fact that our moral circle is expanding, as Singer has argued, and that we can rest in peace in knowing that we are both kind and spiteful; We are ostracized for behaving immorally and often encouraged to treat sentient beings well; And that, with the increasing availability of education and laws, our morality may flourish.

Part B

Our Priorities

Chapter 5

The Human Rights of the Christian

> Christians understand that rights do not come from the Constitution nor are they granted to us by government. Rights are given to us by God. Government's responsibility is to recognize and to protect those rights. –Albert Mohler[1]

In developed countries, we are rarely met with the greatest threats to life, as was typical for our ancestors throughout history. Hunter-gatherers were met with predators when in the wild; Peasants in France in the medieval ages were stricken by plagues that wiped out cities; And, the simplest ailments like a fever made life unbearable for most throughout history.

Today, we rarely send our young to fight our wars, we expect fair trials when accused of breaking the law, and we publicly protest when our governments do not guarantee us the freedoms that we think of as self-evident. It took a long time for these basic rights and freedoms to develop, however. And what is most troubling, is that many in the world do not have the same access to rights because either they are minorities whose expectations about their treatment in the world is met with prejudice or they are in countries that are ruled by autocrats and usurpers that do not care about the interests of the lowly.

Refugees continuously flee from war-torn countries to

Europe and other neighboring nations with more stable economies because of the promise of a better life for their families. More than 780 million people are malnourished around the Globe and approximately 9 million people die annually from starvation. What is most troubling about these numbers is that it has been estimated that if the West collectively decided to challenge famine, they would be able to do so successfully. As a species, we still have a lot of work to do when it comes to guaranteeing everyone their equal share of rights without special treatment depending on race, gender, sexual orientation, religious beliefs, or nationality.

In this chapter, the question I want to address is whether a Christian society, one that is majority Christian, can guarantee humans rights in the best way. Once again, this topic is undoubtedly above this chapter. Still, I wanted to briefly touch on it because I believe that human rights – especially concerning displaced people groups, immigrants, and refugees – is among the most pressing concerns for the 21st century.

I will briefly address some policies that Western countries can adopt, but I will primarily show why Christians have a unique responsibility to house, feed, and sacrifice everyday mundane pleasures of life for the sake of refugees. Indeed, the New Testament provides some compelling reasons for why human life is sacred. Of course, to accept these reasons, we have to admit that God exists, as was pointed out in th chapter on Christian morality. Many will not find this precondition appealing. But I still hope that you attempt to understand what the basic premises of Christian reasoning are on human rights. Maybe we will be able to learn from one another.

Christianity and Human Nature

Any discussion of Christian human rights must begin with the Christian notion of human depravity, or "total depravity," as Reformed theologians put it. This doctrine teaches that we are separated from God because of the Fall of Adam and Eve in the Garden of Eden. The way God handles humans in the Old Testament (think: the flood, Pharaoh, not letting Moses into the Promised Land, the way God deals with His chosen people) was because of this depraved natural state.

For obvious reasons, the idea that humans are fatally depraved led to a lot of injustice in the name of the Church. Bertrand Russell argued that the doctrine of original sin and total depravity was the main difference between Western and Eastern philosophy. Confucius held that men are born good; Aquinas, to put it mildly, did not.[2] For Russell, that meant that in the East, men were "more apt to submit to reason."[3] In the West, Martin Luther outright rejected Aristotle's ethics because Luther could not fathom that human beings could do good or think good without God.[4]

As I've pointed out before, Christianity today bears almost no resemblance to the Christianity of Luther and Calvin, let alone to that of Augustine or Aquinas. Many have even questioned the historical Jesus, stating that he resembles a somewhat foreign Christianity that, for instance, never believed in heaven.[5] Historically, it isn't even easy to settle how much Paul and Jesus agreed upon, creating an exciting pile of scholarly research. In this chapter, I'm putting all these differences in interpretation aside and looking at whether human rights can be defended in Christianity with our understanding of the Bible today.

Christianity and Rights

Christianity certainly contributed to the rights of individuals in the world, even if it has its fair share of horror stories associated with it. Anyone that would argue that religion has only done wrong and that it, in the words of Christopher Hitchens, "poisons everything," is generalizing and blatantly mistaken. In fact, the historian Alvin Schmidt points out that the spread of Christianity led to an impressive number of significant achievements in society. Among which were:

[T]he outlawing of infanticide, child abandonment,

and abortion in the Roman Empire (in AD 374); the abolition of the brutal battles to the death in which thousands of gladiators had died (in 404); the ending of the cruel punishment of branding the faces of criminals (in 315); the institution of prison reforms, such as the segregating of male and female prisoners (by 361); the discontinuation of the practice of human sacrifice among the Irish; the outlawing of pedophilia; the granting of property rights and other protections to women; the banning of polygamy (which is still practiced in some Muslim nations today); the prohibition of the burning alive of widows in India (in 1829); the end of the painful and crippling practice of binding young women's feet in China (in 1912); persuading government officials to begin a system of public schools in Germany (in the 16th century); and advancing the idea of compulsory education of all children in a number of European countries.[6]

We can take each of these at face value and assess their historical validity, but I think it is more worthwhile to accept the obvious: Christianity may have also done some good for the world. However, it is important to clarify that admitting that Christianity brought some good to society is not saying much at all about the validity and utility of religion, in this case, Christianity, or its contribution to human rights. In the end, even World War II did some good for society, namely that it saw an increase in women's equality, by employing them in factories and also in that it brought immense technological advances, contributing to the development of modern computers, for example. Today, these same computers are contributing to the educational advancements in developing countries around the world. Despite some of the good that the War brought to us, few would justify the War as a necessary step for humanity. The good should be mentioned, but it hardly justifies the bad.

As much as Christianity has contributed with some good

to society, which is undeniable, despite the bad, we can also say that Christianity has a history of exclusive morality, at least when it comes to the beliefs of minorities.

Separation of Church and State

Many of the human rights concerns of the Christian I will discuss in this chapter, from abortion, women's rights, LGBTQ+ rights, require a separation of church and state. To put it plainly, the Church has what many think is a distorted view of human morality. The morality of the Christian right is not something that many in the West living in the 21st century are prone to accept. That may be apparent to some readers. What is not transparent is that many readers, even though they acknowledge that we have differences in how we perceive morality, will still seek to institutionalize their morality in law. That is where many secularists rightly object.

Secular thinkers will claim that church and state should be separated in a democratic society that accepts each individual based on their distinct human rights. Indeed, Susan Jacoby explains that "It took 150 years, the Enlightenment, and more instruction in the horror of theocracies in the Old World before the United States of America became the first nation on the planet to uphold the legal separation of church and state."[7] We do not want to get rid of this separation since it took so long to establish.

To reiterate, to live freely with one another, deeply moralized topics such as abortion, same-sex relations, immigration, and traditional family values have to be settled by separating Church dogma and teaching from society. From the way I see it, that would be the only way we can effectively cohabitate. It would be democratically unjust to not allow someone the freedom to express their views, to the same extent that it would be unjust to not allow someone to act out their freedoms, such as to pursue an abortion, to the legal measure allowed in society.

Although, all of these topics that I want to discuss in this chapter come with many nuances and exceptions. I do not expect to do them any justice here. I want to simply touch on some of the human rights concerns that the Christian right allows for and show the overarching theme that could help us in society get past our differences and learn to cohabitate.

In America, the separation of church and state in the Constitution, even if it was only on the federal level, allowed some evangelical denominations, including the methodists and baptists, to spread the Gospel without limits despite the presence of established churches in many states, as was the case in Connecticut and Virginia, for example.[8] Frances FitzGerald writes in *The Evangelicals: The Struggle to Shape America*, that the American Constitution "created a marketplace of religion, giving all denominations and sects an incentive to increase their flocks, and beginning a process that made America the most religious country in the developed world."[9]

Surprisingly, or unsurprisingly, the influence of Christianity in politics in America fluctuates depending on religious involvement in state affairs and vice versa. At the beginning of the nineteenth century, more than 200 years ago, America was marked by a tremendously influential evangelical community. Christians "dominated" all cultural institutions, public schools, and universities; In fact, Fitzgerald explains that, "In this period there was no real distinction between religion and politics."[10]

Fast forward 160 years later, and Christian influence in American politics starts to deteriorate. By the 1960s and '70s, a Catholic becomes president (a seemingly impossible divide between Protestants and Catholics breached), the Supreme Court ban prayer and Bible-reading in schools, social reformers start the civil rights movement, citizens flock the Washington Monument and the White House to protest against the Vietnam War, and the Supreme Court passes *Roe v. Wade*, making abortion a constitutional right.[11]

Because of the rapid decline of Christian influence in the '60s in America, many today seem to forget that the Republican Party was not always as closely knit with the Christian right and the evangelical community as it is today. We think of the Republican party as the evangelical party because of Donald Trump's victory in the federal election in 2016, where he boasted over 81 percent of the evangelical vote.[12] It was not always so, however. It was not until Richard Nixon's presidency that the Christian right became mobilized for personal political gain.

Consider the fact that Billy Graham, one of the most popular evangelists in American history, and the "pastor to presidents," has given spiritual counsel to presidents from Harry S. Truman to Barack Obama. The question is, why would these presidents need spiritual counsel in the first place in a country that has separated church from politics? Indeed, Billy Graham, ever fearful of the moral impact on America if Christianity lost its overbearing presence in the public space, would often urge America to repent because of their sins. In one of his impactful sermons, he called on Americans: *"Repent ye! Repent ye! . . . There is no alternative! If Sodom and Gomorrah could not get away with sin, if Pompeii and Rome could not escape, neither can Los Angeles! . . . If we don't have a revival . . . in the next month or next year, we might not have any more time. Like Israel in the time of Isaiah, America is drifting away from God."*[13]

Graham's close acquaintance, President Dwight D. Eisenhower, was among those impacted by Graham's call for repentance and even made a connection between the "personal faith" of American citizens and the potential "health of the nation." President Woodrow Wilson similarly claimed that America is the last spiritual hope for the world at large. Hugh Lamb, the Catholic bishop of Philadelphia, called democracy without God, "an empty word"; Lewis Mumford, a cultural critic, argued that religion served as an "absolute standard" to "measure social policies and correct the course of the state."[14] The theme was consistent across the American evangelical community and the Christian right in America in the latter half of the 20th century.

Eisenhower regularly used religious rhetoric in public life, more than any other president before him. Under his presidency, Eisenhower instituted national prayer breakfasts, Congress added the phrase "under God" to the Pledge of Allegiance and "In God We Trust" on the currency, making it a national motto. Unsurprisingly, this granted Eisenhower favor from the evangelical community. Indeed, the Republican National Committee in 1955 called Eisenhower, "not only the political leader but the spiritual leader of our times."[15]

Other presidents followed suit. The Democratic presidential nominee, Jimmy Carter, a devout Southern Baptist, often spoke of his "born-again" experience, which was popularized by Billy Graham at his signature revivals. President Gerald Ford, an Episcopalian, similarly described himself as born-again and was the first American president to directly address the Southern Baptist Convention (SBC), an influential Christian denomination of the Christian right[16]

Few predicted the influence of the Christian right in politics. Indeed, Fitzgerald writes that "The eruption of the Christian right was sudden."[17] Political observers were shocked by the political influence of the Christian right in the 1980s.[18] "After all, John F. Kennedy, and most recently Jimmy Carter ... had drawn bright lines between their religious beliefs and their public commitments."[19] Despite this theoretical separation of church and state, reality proved a bleak picture for secularists and moderates that thought that religious persuasion ought to be a personal affair.

The Christian right in America in the 1990s was rooted in churches, influencing state school boards when it came to strictly Christian education and science-denial (Creationism), but also in limiting access to abortion. One of the strongest voices and forces against the legalization of abortion in America was who Fitzgerald calls "the most curious and contradictory of all the Christian right leaders," Pat Robertson.[20] Robertson was the "standard-bearer" for the Christian Coalition movement at its political height from 1987 to 1998. After Bill

Clinton's election, the Coalition experienced unprecedented growth in both membership and financing.[21] Robertson even argued that the U.S. Constitution did not say anything about the separation of church and state and that America had "fallen away" from the faith of the Founding Fathers.[22]

It was arguably because of the Christian right's hatred of Bill Clinton and his, for the time progressive wife, Hillary, that the Coalition experienced such growth. It went from 250,000 to 1.6 million members in three years, amassing an annual budget of $25 million.[23] In the early 2000s, President George W. Bush understood the Christian right's political importance, along with his political strategist Karl Rove, and surrounded himself with conservative Christians.[24] Forty percent of his staff regularly attended prayer meetings and Bible studies in the White House.[25] Bush also formed the Office of Faith-Based Initiatives, which took federal money and fueled religious social service providers.[26] Fitzgerald writes, "To many Democrats and moderate Republicans, the White House and the Republican leadership had seemed to have become a captive of the Christian right. To many evangelicals, the opposite seemed to be the case: the Christian right had become a function of Republican politics."[27]

Needless to say, when religion is closely tied to the state, bad things follow, not only for the state but also for religious influence. When institutionalized, "atheism" was similarly harmful to the freedoms of citizens, as could be seen in the "secularizing" process of the USSR. When it came to Christianity's influence in America, the Christian involvement in politics created noticeable social resentment in the late 2000s. In 2008, 45 percent of people agreed that religious leaders, such as Rick Warren or Billy Graham, should not try to influence voting, an increase by 15 percent from 1991.[28] Eric Kaufmann writes in *Whiteshift* that "[T]he overreach of the religious right seemed to have accelerated a trend towards secularization among Millennial Americans."[29] Indeed we can see this trend in the increase of Americans that never attended religious services from 15 percent in 1995 to 22 percent in 2008.[30]

Along with the public's increasing denouncement of Christian involvement in politics, intellectuals took to pen and paper to advocate for more separation between church and state. Books criticizing religion were growing in popularity across America. These books included, *American Fascists: The Christian Right and the War on America* by Chris Hedges, *The End of Faith* by Sam Harris, *The God Delusion* by Richard Dawkins, *Religion Poisons Everything* by Christopher Hitchens, and *Breaking the Spell* by Daniel C. Dennett. Fitzgerald explains that toward the end of Bush's presidency, "the political landscape had changed"; "The Republicans had lost control of the Congress, and the Christian right for the first time faced challenges from within the evangelical community."[31]

The Christian right understandably felt some resentment toward their weakening influence in state affairs. Some Christian thinkers assured the Christian public that they should not be disappointed. In *The Myth of a Christian Nation,* revered Gregory A. Boyd, the head of a large conservative church in St. Paul, Minnesota, argued that America could never become a "Christian nation" in the first place.[32] Boyd argued that Christ's kingdom was "not of this world"; that the Constitution never hinted at establishing a Christian nation, and that America never resembled the "domain of God." He warned that evangelicals in America falsely see themselves as "moral guardians," and end up making certain "minor" sins into "major" sins because of this. Boyd pointed out that the Bible mentions divorce and remarriage more than same-sex marriage and that focusing on same-sex marriage is "self-serving." Most importantly, Boyd pointed out that Paul taught that he could never judge those outside of the Church since they are not held accountable for the same sins as members of Christ's body. That is not to say that Christians are not to witness to unbelievers or share their moral convictions but instead that they should not enforce "their righteous will on others."[33]

Boyd's convictions for the separation of church and state

were not as popular with the Christian right who thought that their weakening political influence meant that their freedoms would be tampered with, if not outright abolished. Indeed, many evangelicals thought President Barack Obama's election in 2008, was a crushing blow, or in the words of SBC leader, Albert Mohler, an "unmitigated disaster."[34] Fitzgerald points out that the political victories of the Democrats would often provoke "end times rhetoric."[35]

Glenn Beck, the popular Christian radio host, even called on his audience to buy farmland and guns and pull their kids from public schools in light of Obama's election.[36] Billy Graham's son, Franklin Graham, blamed Obama for the moral downfall of America, and for "pluralism," callously stating that, "The President is leading the nation on a sinful course, and God will judge him and us as a nation if we don't repent."[37] James Dobson argued that the traditional family "will likely crumble, presaging the fall of Western civilization."[38]

These calls can be explained by what sociologists call a "Reconstructionist ideology" of "dominionism," the belief that "Christians had a God-given right to rule all earthly institutions."[39] If you really believed that the Creator of the Universe divinely orchestrated your morals, then little is stopping you from forcing your beliefs on others. In the end, these morals and understanding the Gospel, are a matter of life and death. Or at least, that is how they are perceived from the Christian right. Arguably, this type of dominionism was the same logic that applied to the colonization of developing nations by the Christian West from the 1600s to the 1900s. And that should certainly trouble us.

Intolerance in Christian Discourse Today

Today, we see similar "end times rhetoric" that Fitzgerald mentioned above in discussions concerning the everyday American culture wars on immigration and race. The conservative Christian writer, John Zmirak, goes so far to say in his article "Systemic Racism and Other Conspiracy Theories" that the sexual revolution of the '60s in America "destroyed the family." In the same article, he calls the Black Lives Matter movement a "Marxist cult," calling every patriotic American and Christian never to dare take a knee in solidarity with the movement.

The speech Zmirak exhibits here is not typically Christian, of course. It is hyper-political more than it is Christian. In Zmirak's world, one that others like Eric Metaxas, Wayne Grudem, Franklin Graham, and Mike Pence share, the rights of those we disagree with should be restricted because they are fundamentally causing harm to the collective morality of society.[40]

In reality, many of the issues that conservative Christians and the Christian right are deeply troubled with are not as harmful as they suppose. We should be skeptical of these intrinsic fears. Studies have repeatedly shown that many of the things we are worried about are greatly exaggerated in our imaginations. Reality is often less scary than the stories we tell ourselves.

For example, citizens across most societies are remarkably bad at guessing the prevalence of teen pregnancy among teens. According to studies conducted by Bobby Duffy, the public in Germany presumed that teenage pregnancy was at 16 percent when, in reality, it was at 0.6 percent. In other words, the public thought that 1 in 6 girls become pregnant annually when, in fact, the number is closer to 1 in 166 girls.[41] In America, the public assumed that teen pregnancy was at 24 percent when, in reality, it was only at 2 percent.[42] The same trend applies to poorer countries such as Brazil, where high school dropout rates among teens are more common than in more developed nations.

In his book, *The Storytelling Animal,* Jonathan Gottschall explains why we exaggerate the societal issues such as the one mentioned above. Gottschall argues that fictitious problems in society help prevent supposed societal disasters. In the end, it is better to be wrong about behavior in society than to not think about it at all. "We're storytelling animals who remember vivid anecdotes far more readily than boring statistics, and some stories are more attractive to the human brain than others."[43] And Christianity is certainly very good at telling these vivid stories that stay in memory.

Now that we touched on some of the history of the separation of church and state in America, or lack thereof, I want to touch on some of the human rights concerns that I believe are among the most pressing for the Christian in the 21st century. Every one of the topics that I will discuss below are very difficult and could have lengthy volumes written on them. For our purposes here, I will discuss them primarily in relation to how Christians and atheists will be able to cohabitate during the 21st century. The first step to do so would be to accept each other's differences. I will also reiterate that the beliefs I will present below are not my own and that some Christians have similarly discarded them. I am presenting the conservative fundamentalist views on all these topics. First, let's discuss the heated topic of abortion.

Abortion

For Christians, humans are made in God's image, along with their depravity, there is inherent worth to a human being. Thus, the secular and atheist observers should understand that when pro-life individuals are protesting abortion, they do not differentiate between the intrinsic value in the adult life and the value in the potential for life in a fetus in the womb; they are both inherently valuable to an almost equal extent.

The urgency of many of these pro-life protestors may seem bizarre to many atheists, but they should once again realize the depth of the pain that these protestors feel. The World Health Organization estimates that annually there are anywhere from 40-50 million abortions in the world, which is approximately 125,000 abortions per day.[44] Needless to say, if you thought that many babies were being killed annually, you would probably be correct to be up in arms about it, even uncivil, God forbid.

The most common Bible verse that is invoked in defense of pro-life views is found in Psalm 139:13-16

I praise you, for I am fearfully and wonderfully made. Wonderful are your works; my soul knows it very well. My frame was not hidden from you, when I was being made in secret, intricately woven in the depths of the earth. Your eyes saw my unformed substance; in your book were written, every one of them, the days that were formed for me, when as yet there was none of them.

Other passages that stress the same include Exodus 21:22-25; Psalm 127:3; Isaiah 44:24; Jeremiah 1:5; and Ephesians 1:7. When thinking about abortion, the Christian right will argue that the inherent sacredness of the fetus (Gen 1:27) outweighs any of the reasons anyone can pose for wanting an abortion, apart from a few exceptions, such as a severe risk to the mother's health.

Biblical Christians who hold the pro-life view on abortion will stress that we should understand the reasons people have abortions in the first place which can garner compassion for the individual. The Christian right, if following the calls of the Bible to live in peace with others (Hebrews 12:14), will show care first and foremost to the woman who chooses abortion if they are truly following God's call to be His "ambassadors" on earth (2 Cor 5:20).

The rest of the Christian community, including the moderates, socially liberal Christians, and others, will see that society reaps benefits from pluralism. If it weren't for the fact that the Christian right thinks of abortion as murder, there would indeed be every reason to object to their steadfast protests of abortion.

There are many philosophical and scientific reasons to object to the pro-life view of abortion. I do not want to do that here. As Joshua Greene writes in *Moral Tribes*, both camps have difficult questions to answer concerning abortion, and they are challenging to dismiss. Both pro-life and pro-choice camps will have to learn how to cohabitate. Until then, it is only right to allow both sides the freedoms they wish for, those that do not think of abortion as murder, the right to abort, and those that do, the right to protest legalization.

It will be very difficult for the Christian right to focus on other issues over abortion since, as I mentioned above, 40-50 million abortions take place each year. We should sympathize with these concerns but urge Christians to consult the science and reconsider the biblical exegesis of these texts as other socially liberal Christians and evangelical moderates have. It doesn't seem like the world is about to change back to the morality of the Christian right of the 1980s in America. Although, I could be wrong about that. The trend in America and across the Globe seems to be running away from the Christian right. It is as Mohler put it in the wake of Obama's election in 2008:

> It's not that our message – we think abortion is wrong, we think same-sex marriage is wrong – didn't get out. It did get out. It's that the entire moral landscape has changed. An increasingly secularized America understands our positions and has rejected them.[45]

Women Rights

There are different strands of feminist evangelicalism within Christianity, but to mention all of these is above this short book. For the Christian right, man and woman are created equal in the Bible (Gen 1:27), but they are not the same in every sense of the word; Hence, they are called "complementarian." That means that for the Christian right, men and women have drastically different roles within the Church but are equal in God's eyes. Peter, for example, writes:

> Likewise, wives, be subject to your own husbands, so that even if some do not obey the word, they may be won without a word by the conduct of their wives, when they see your respectful and pure conduct. Do not let your adorning be external—the braiding of

hair and the putting on of gold jewelry, or the cloth-ing you wear— but let your adorning be the hidden person of the heart with the imperishable beauty of a gentle and quiet spirit, which in God's sight is very precious. For this is how the holy women who hoped in God used to adorn themselves, by submitting to their own husbands, as Sarah obeyed Abraham, call-ing him lord. And you are her children, if you do good and do not fear anything that is frightening. Likewise, husbands, live with your wives in an understanding way, showing honor to the woman as the weaker ves-sel, since they are heirs with you of the grace of life, so that your prayers may not be hindered. 1 Pet 3:1-7

Nowadays, anyone that would speak this way to women would either be banned from university campuses or wholly ostracized from society. Peter's writing needs to be understood in the context that it was written in. In a way, the call for any-one, both man and woman, to "adorn" themselves with a "gen-tle and quiet spirit" is an honorable call. However, the demand for gentleness should not be unique to women. In this passage, it certainly seems that women are uniquely called to this meek behavior. But one should be reminded that this "meekness" was also seen in Christ and that each Christian is called to resemble Him. Paul urges the Corinthians with the "meekness and gentle-ness" of Christ (2 Cor 10:1). Jesus repeatedly says that he came to serve, not to be served (Luke 22:27). Christ is both "gentle" and "humble" (Mat 11:29); He washes the feet of His disciples (John 13:5) and asks God to "forgive" those who crucified Him (Luke 23:34). So, when Peter calls on women to be "respectful," "pure," and "gentle," critics should also point out that this same gentle-ness was seen in Christ and that this behavior should be seen in all Christians. Of course, these are not the only admonishments in the Bible that call on women to act in a unique way. Paul, in 1 Timothy 2:11-15 writes:

Let a woman learn quietly with all submissiveness. I

do not permit a woman to teach or to exercise authority over a man; rather, she is to remain quiet. For Adam was formed first, then Eve; and Adam was not deceived, but the woman was deceived and became a transgressor. Yet she will be saved through childbearing—if they continue in faith and love and holiness, with self-control.

This passage is much more challenging to understand and interpret for today's world. Conservative Christians will stand by it because Scripture is without error, and all of it is inspired by God (2 Tim 3:16). Some Christians take these passages too seriously and make seriously sexist remarks in conjunction with them. Wayne Grudem makes one notable faulty conclusion based on these texts in *Christian Ethics* where he writes:

In our marriage, Margaret and I talk frequently and at length about many decisions. Sometimes these are large decisions (such as buying a house or a car), and sometimes they are small decisions (such as where we should go for a walk together). I often defer to her wishes, and she often defers to mine, because we love each other. . . . But in every decision, whether large or small, and whether we have reached agreement or not, the responsibility to make the decision still rests with me. . . . I do not agree with those who say that male headship makes a difference only once in 10 years or so, when a husband and wife can't reach agreement. I think that male headship makes a difference in *every decision* that a couple makes every day of their married life.[46]

Grudem further writes that a woman in marriage has a "quiet, subtle acknowledgment" that the decisions are made by the husband, "not the wife."[47] He explains, that this responsibility is not because of some intrinsic wisdom that men have, it is only because God gave men that responsibility. He concludes,

"In the face of cultural pressures to the contrary, I will not forsake this male headship; I will not deny it; and I will not be embarrassed by it."[48]

John Piper explains the complementarian concept and the many nuances accompanied with it in his book, *Recovering Biblical Manhood and Womanhood*, which he co-authored with Wayne Grudem. For myself, I believe that the sexist remarks in connection to this teaching are plentiful. Thus, this teaching does seem to do more harm than good in society. But, our rights granted by international law to assemble should be given to Christians. And if they want to teach this then the Christian right can and is entirely in their right to do so. It seems that we once again must abandon our prejudices, urge slow reasoning, and interpret the argument we disagree with in the way they do to find peace and common ground with one another.

Gay Rights

As I hope to have shown in the previous chapter on Christian morality, the Bible is clear on whether same-sex relations are a sin. Historically speaking, those who were attracted to the same sex were far from treated equally by the Church, so it seems that guaranteeing minorities the rights they deserve was not a high priority throughout Christendom.

For our purposes here, I will touch on whether the Christian right has a way of providing those who are attracted to the same-sex an equal place within society today. The only way, as I see it, for the entire LGBTQ+ community to have a place among the Christian right, is if Christians repurpose their commitment from keeping the commandments in the Word of God to a loving embrace of everyone, no matter the arbitrary "sinfulness" of their actions.

However, Christians should not make "minor" sins into "major" sins, as was pointed out above by Boyd. Those who masturbate have a place in the Church, but it is also true that they, if unrepentant, will not inherit the Kingdom of God, as is clearly stated in the Bible (Mat 5:27-30). It is not that deeds save, but rather that "good trees" will bear fruit. It seems that the only way the gay community will gain precedence in the Christian world is if Christians make weak arguments concerning same-sex relations in the Bible.

For example, the author of *God and the Gay Christian*, Matthew Vines, says that the term "homosexual" did not exist until 1892 and that the Bible could not have therefore commented on homosexual practices. And although the term may not have existed in the English language, the Bible clearly rejects same-sex behavior. Vines simply states that the Bible rejects "lustful" same-sex behavior.[49] Therefore, it seems that the only way gay individuals find acceptance in the Church among the Christian right and biblical Christians is if the Church starts reinterpreting statements in this manner.

The Christian right that sticks to the original texts and their meaning will have to live in a society where they agree to disagree with liberal Christians and many atheists on same-sex relations. Once again, the separation between church and state is necessary. This would mean that we would have to give religious believers the freedom to believe what secular thinkers consider "intolerant" or unethical. In an ideal world, everyone would agree with us on the freedoms that we give to each citizen. But, in reality, we do not live in a perfect world and have to compromise with one another.

The trend of societal acceptance of "homosexuality" suggests that the Christian right will have to accept this change. In 2017, 64 percent of Americans were in favor of same-sex marriage, whereas in 1996, only 27 percent were in favor of it.[50] The trend seems to be shifting in favor of those who advocate for same-sex marriage.

I have discussed abortion, women's rights, and gay rights. In all of these, we notice the problems that the lack of separation of church and state poses for society. Simply put, we will never be able to agree on all moral issues. When we disagree with one another on these issues, we should recognize what I discussed in Chapter Two, that our intuitions often take over our better nature. There are many reasons we think the way we do, and some of these reasons are uniquely challenging to discard.

In *The Happiness Hypothesis*, Jonathan Haidt for example explains that "[L]iberals are experts in thinking about issues of victimization, equality, autonomy, and the rights of individuals, particularly those of minorities and nonconformists. Conservatives, on the other hand, are experts in thinking about loyalty to the group, respect for authority and tradition, and sacredness."[51] Most of the issues that we discussed are nuanced and require historical, statistical, and philosophical analysis. Because of their complexity and our intuitions, we should be compassionate in how we disagree with each other.

Ethnic Minorities

Lastly, I would like to briefly discuss the question of how Christian America dealt with their ethnic minorities, especially the African-American community. In the United States, the abolitionist movement had both Christian and secular defenders. Grudem writes that there were, of course, Christian "vocal defenders" of slavery in the South, but that "they were vastly outnumbered by the many Christians who were ardent abolitionists, speaking, writing, and agitating constantly for the abolition of slavery."[52]

Alvin Schmidt estimates that two-thirds of American abolitionists were Christian clergymen, most notable of which were Elijah Lovejoy, Lyman Beecher, Edward Beecher, Harriet Beecher Stowe, Charles Finney, Charles T. Torrey, Theodore Weld, and William Lloyd Garrison.[53]

What Grudem fails to mention, however, is that the 17th century was not as eventful for Christian anti-slavery speech. The British historian, Hugh Thomas in *The Slave Trade: The Story of the Atlantic Slave Trade, 1440-1870* writes that in fact "There is no record in the seventeenth century of any preacher who, in any sermon, whether in the Cathedral of Saint-Andre in

Bordeaux or a Presbyterian meeting house in Liverpool, condemned the trade in black slaves."[54]

Fast forward three hundred years and Martin Luther King Jr., a Christian pastor, leads the American civil-rights movement that undeniably helped end a lot of segregation and prejudice in the United States.[55] So, the literature is mixed on this. Both the secular and Christian camps have juxtaposing views on history. I aim at providing a balanced account in this book, and in reality, the world is often quite convoluted. It is disheartening that many think of the world in terms of black and white: some Christians favored abolishing the slave trade, and some Christians were against it.

The connection between one's faith and actions is not as straightforward as Grudem and Schmidt would have us believe. Just because someone is Christian and acts morally does not necessarily mean that they were guided by their religion to act in that way. Adolf Hitler professed to be Christian, does that mean that his faith influenced his vitriolic hatred of Jews? I would like to think not. Historians are divided, however. Christianity and antisemitism are historically linked. This hatred can be traced back to Christianity, but the Bible's teaching does not condone it. Although, even that is disputed, depending on your preconceived biases concerning this issue. In the same way, we should not hastily presume that Christians who act morally exceptionally for the time they're in do so because of their faith. The connection is possible, but not automatic.

Another problem with making sweeping judgments about history and religion is that cultural or complacent Christianity (the act of being Christian simply because you were born into a Christian household) was common throughout the medieval ages because there was simply no one but Christians in most of Europe. Atheism was not an acceptable worldview for a very long time and religious minorities were persecuted. Atheists were still not allowed university positions in the time of David Hume, and can still to this day not run for president in the United States, at least not publicly. The majority of America was Caucasian and Christian in the 18th century, and hence the racism in it would be undeniable.

Of course some abolitionists were Christian – the majority of America and England was Christian. The more important question concerning the future treatment of ethnic minorities by biblical Christians is in what the Bible teaches about slavery. Secular critics will have a tough time showing why and how Christians can justify slavery via the Bible.

Some did justify slavery with the Bible, but, for the most part, these seem to be mistakes in interpretation. In fact, the institution of slavery is completely thwarted by the Bible (Exodus 21:16; 1 Cor 7:21; 1 Tim 1:10). Let's have a look at some of the texts that slave-owners used to justify slavery:

> When a man strikes his slave, male or female, with a rod and the slave dies under his hand, he shall be avenged. But if the slave survives a day or two, he is not to be avenged, for the slave is his money. Exodus 21:20-21

> As for your male and female slaves whom you may have: you may buy male and female slaves from among the nations that are around you. You may also buy from among the strangers who sojourn with you and their clans that are with you, who have been born in your land, and they may be your property. You may bequeath them to your sons after you to inherit as a possession forever. You may make slaves of them, but over your brothers the people of Israel you shall not rule, one over another ruthlessly. Lev 25:44-46

> Slaves are to be submissive to their own masters in everything; they are to be well-pleasing, not argumentative, not pilfering, but showing all good faith, so that in everything they may adorn the doctrine of God our Savior. Titus 2:9-10

Slaves, obey your earthly masters with fear and trem-
bling, with a sincere heart, as you would Christ. Eph
6:5

Servants, be subject to your masters with all respect,
not only to the good and gentle but also to the unjust.
1 Pet 2:18

There is neither Jew nor Greek, there is neither slave
nor free, there is no male and female, for you are all
one in Christ Jesus. Gal 3:28

For freedom Christ has set us free; stand firm therefore, and do not submit again to a yoke of slavery. Gal
5:1

Typically, Christian evangelicals today will not turn to
the Old Testament to see how to behave as a Christian because
Jesus came to fulfill the Law and create a New Covenant with
His people. So, citing the Old Testament as a justification for
slavery, or as a criticism against Christianity, does not do much.
There are plenty of things in the Old Testament that should be
interpreted as specific cultural instances and not as precursors
for behavior today. At least, this is one way Christians can discard these harmful passages. Although, it is more difficult to see
why we should keep the other ones, but we touched on that in
previous chapters.

Furthermore, the Bible teaches that "[God] made from one
man every nation of humankind" (Acts 17:26). Jesus himself
finds the faith of a Roman, not an Israeli, greater than that of
anyone in Israel (Mat 8:5-13). And, finally, when Jesus calls on
his disciples to spread the Gospel, He says that they should go to
the ends of the earth, to "all nations" (Mat 28:18-20). The Bible,
therefore, Christian thinkers claim, is more inclusive to those of
other races. In the end, God wants Christians to be an "alternate
city" (Mat 5:14-17) because there is neither Greek nor Jew (Gal
3:28). Therefore, we can safely conclude that slavery is not read-

ily condoned in the Bible, as critics suggest it is.

It should also be pointed out that the "slavery" discussed in the New Testament, for example, and slavery in America were of drastically different characteristics. Murray Harris summarizes these differences in *Slave of Christ: A New Testament Metaphor for Total Devotion to Christ*:

> In the first century, slaves were not distinguishable from free persons by race, by speech, or by clothing; they were sometimes more highly educated than their owners and held responsible professional positions; some persons sold themselves into slavery for economic or social advantage; they could reasonably hope to be emancipated after 10 or 20 years of service or by their 30s at the latest; they were not denied the right of public assembly and were not socially segregated (at least in the cities); they could accumulate savings to buy their freedom; their natural inferiority was not assumed.[56]

Hence, the connection between biblical teaching and slavery is vacuous and merely a mistake in interpretation.

Immigration, Human Rights, and Right-wing Populists

The next topic I want to discuss is immigration. Christians are particularly compelled by the life of Jesus Christ himself to give to the homeless and displaced. Christians have every reason to give to the poor and to the distressed not only in the country they are in but to societies across the Globe that need it most.

The conservative estimate on the future of refugees due to climate change alone is that by 2050 there will be more than 140 million migrants.[57] I say conservative estimate because some estimates put the number of migrants closer to 200 million and up to 1 billion by 2050, estimated by the United Nations' International Organization for Migration.[58] That number does seem relatively high, however, and unlikely. We will just have to see how things turn out to know whether these estimates are accurate. Nonetheless, even the fact that these estimates are so high in the first place is good enough reason to do something about it. The more conservative estimate from the World Bank in 2018 is that if emissions and warming stay at their present trajectory, sub-Saharan Africa will produce 86 million climate migrants; South Asia, 40 million; and Latin America, 17 million.[59]

In today's society, immigration is frowned upon and even taboo, so Christians will have a difficult time defending their views against the dogmatism of, unfortunately, most conservative political parties in the world. There are a few reasons why right-wing parties are connected to anti-immigrant speech.

Today, anti-immigration rhetoric is typically associated with (1) "Eurabia" discourse where Western or liberal values are deemed threatened by the influx of Muslim migrants and (2) the resurgence of populist right-wing parties in Western countries. When it comes to Eurabia discourse, Niall Ferguson and other writers in the early 2000s popularized the notion that Europe's increasing Muslim population would eventually cause serious threats to the liberal values of the West. Their arguments rely on the widely disputed premise that Europe will become majority-Muslim as early as 2050 or 2100.[60] These fears seem to be overblown, however.

The emergence of right-wing populism is a more pressing and immediate threat. It should garner more attention from us since its prevalence in politics directly affects the policies on immigration. Simply defined, right-wing populism is the populist struggle against the established left-leaning elite class that controls the media, academia, and most mainstream discussions in politics. Right-wing populists are also associated with anti-immigration, anti-Europe, anti-liberalization, and anti-globalization rhetoric. Furthermore, right-wing populists are concerned with culture and preserving it in the West and so it makes some sense that they are overtly focused on immigration.[61] In fact, Kaufmann and Matthew Goodwin conducted a meta-analysis of thirty-five studies between 1995 and 2016 and found that twenty-seven countries had a connection between views on immigration and support for the populist-right, stating that the connection was "virtually identical."[62]

In Western Europe, populist-right parties became more prevalent in the 1980s and saw increasing support in the following fifteen years.[63] Elsewhere in the world, the trends are similar. Jair Bolsonaro, the current President of Brazil, known for his fierce advocacy of social conservatism, credited his win in Brazil's election to his adamant respect for "families, principles, traditions, customs, . . . our culture, and religion."[64] Austria, Switzerland, and Ireland, which are less receptive to same-sex relations, are also less positive about immigration than socially liberal Sweden, Denmark, and the Netherlands.[65]

Another notable right-wing populist, the Hungarian President, Viktor Orban, said that immigration "only means trouble and danger to the European people."[66] Orban further spewed that Hungary will "teach Brussels, the human traffickers, and the migrants that Hungary is a sovereign country," and subsequently constructed a fence on the Serbian border trapping migrants in Greece.[67] For the right-wing populists, taking care of the nation's self-interest is of primary concern; the estimated 79.5 million forcibly displaced people worldwide (2019) are not.[68]

The world is becoming increasingly hostile to refugees because right-wing populists occupy its shores. Arguably, one of the most pressing ways to serve the poor is not simply to feed them but to house them in democracies and provide adequate shelter in safe refugee camps. The Bible repeatedly calls to feed, serve, and love the poor. But the question is whether we can do more here, perhaps something more tangible and concrete.

Solutions to Immigration

Kaufmann writes that one feasible solution for dealing with immigration effectively is the construction of long-term refugee camps in countries that border with conflict zones, such as the ones in Kenya and Lebanon.[69] We could also construct camps like these in European democracies, because, in his words, "If we are serious about the principle of offering a safe haven to those fleeing for their lives, we must accept this responsibility."[70] Kaufmann further writes that the West should allow the free transportation of refugees from conflict areas to the EU, resulting in fewer deaths at sea, more refuge, and safer conditions in migrant facilities.[71] He argues that the funds for this project should come from the international community through charities and donations from wealthier countries, including those in the Persian Gulf and East Asia.[72]

Christian charities have done work like this before. The already mentioned popular Christian leader, Rick Warren, started what he called a "PEACE" plan in light of the tremendous economic success of his Christian self-help book, *The Purpose Driven Life*. Forbes estimated that by 2006, only a few years after its launch, the book made approximately $25 million. With its success, Warren thought it necessary and worthwhile to focus on "the biggest problems on the planet."[73] His PEACE plan stood for:

- Plant new churches (later, 'partner with churches' or 'promote reconciliation')
- Equipe servant-leaders
- Assist the poor
- Care for the sick
- Educate the next generation

When asked about his PEACE plan, Warren said that he had been enlightened by Psalm 72, where King Solomon prayed for guidance in supporting widows and orphans.[74] Warren admitted that he rarely thought about the poor before that day of personal revelation in his life. In his words, "I've had four years in Greek and Hebrew and I've got doctorates. How did I miss the 2,000 verses in the Bible where it talks about the poor?"[75] Hopefully, other influential Christians are enlightened in similar ways.

For obvious reasons, Christian charities should consider it a priority to house, educate, and feed refugees, along with the rest of the world, because by all accounts, the number of refugees in the world is only about to increase. And we are far too slow in our response.

This chapter looked at the importance of separating church and state, establishing a secular state to effectively resolve our moral differences between the Christian right and other socially liberal citizens. Then we looked at specific reasons that immigration should be focused on by Christians because of God's call to feed the poor and care for the sick. Biblically – not historically – we have seen that Christians pose value to the individual and can justify treating others with the rights they deserve in the 21st century. To do that, they will have to put aside their moral differences with others to cohabitate with those who disagree with them on these difficult moral issues.

Chapter 6

The Human Rights
of the Atheist

God *is* dead – it's just taking a while to get rid of the body. – Yuval Noah Harari[1]

If God does not exist, everything is permitted. – Fyodor Dostoevsky

This statement, often associated with the Russian novelist, Fyodor Dostoevsky, though never actually written by him, encapsulates some of the ways some theists view atheism and what they think is its necessary correlation with nihilism.[2] It has been extensively quoted by theologians and apologists alike. It has also often been invoked by believers when reminded that the world is becoming more secular. If the world is more secular, what stops people from infringing on other people's rights? If our values are arbitrary, evolved by chance, how can our rights be universal and guaranteed equally? For the Christian, the answer is they cannot.

From Ben Shapiro, Jordan Peterson, Ravi Zacharias, to Eric Metaxas, and many other popular contemporary thinkers, the Western world, which in theory (and reality, to some extent) harnesses the values of liberty and free speech for all, is directly descended from Judeo-Christian principles. Without Judaism and Christianity, they claim, we would have never achieved the intellectual, moral, and human rights progress most now enjoy in Western society.

Indeed, we should appreciate the progress society has made in human rights. Today, we find a lot of commonplace behavior in the past as barbaric, inhumane, and disgusting. For instance, up until 150 years ago, children regularly watched public hangings and executions. Few criticized capital punishment because few thought there were problems with it.[3] Torture and scoldings were standard practices adopted by every civilization throughout history from the Assyrians, Persians, Seleucids, Romans, Chinese, Aztecs, to the Hindus. Steven Pinker explains in his book, *Better Angels of Our Nature: Why Violence Has Declined* that "*all* of the first complex civilizations were absolutist theocracies which punished victimless crimes with torture and mutilation."[4] When Christians discuss God's universal moral compass, they should then explain the universality of torture and indignance to suffering.

The rights and values we adopted today are radically different from those of our predecessors. As Pinker explains, throughout medieval Europe, "scores of trivial affronts and infractions were punishable by death."[5] These trivial offenses included: "sodomy, gossiping, stealing cabbages, picking up sticks on the Sabbath, talking back to parents, and criticizing the royal garden."[6]

Today, we rightly think of these offenses as minor, and because of our better grasp of psychology and human behavior, excuse them readily. In the past, people were not so lucky. The atrocitologist R. J. Rummel claims that between Jesus' time and the 20th century, "19 million people were executed for trivial offenses."[7]

In the previous chapter, I attempted to show the best side of the Christian argument for human rights. Here, I am showing the argument of the opposition. I will try to do so in a balanced way, nonetheless.

Universal Human Rights in the Bible

From the previous chapter, we know that Christians have some way of defending human rights biblically. If humans were made in the image of God, then surely we should treat them well. But Christians have one difficult hurdle they must overcome if they are to defend human rights consistently. And that is the discrepancy over the call to "love your neighbor" in both the Old and New Testaments. It is not only that Christianity has the historical problem of locating these universal human rights and values that they champion; They also have a difficult time defending the exegesis of the texts concerning the love for their neighbors. In fact, there is a lot of disagreement over how far the neighborly love in the Bible extends.

Many scholars rightly point out that the values that Christians claim are "universal" are situated, exclusive, and temporary. Robert Wright, in his book, *The Evolution of God*, makes a compelling case for Jesus not being as loving as we presume; And, instead, that Paul, "the apostle of love," was primarily the one responsible for promoting the "loving" message of Christianity. Originally, Christian love was a "brotherly love" or "familial love."[8] Wright elaborates: "familial love is by definition discerning – it is directed inwardly, not outwardly; toward kin, not toward everyone."[9] Wright argues that one of the key components to Christianity's success as a religion was that it rewarded those who became Christians by granting them this "brotherly love." Thus, the original appeal of Christianity was that it provided whoever joined the religion, the "benefits of an extended family," which included financial and material assistance when needed.[10]

The idea to love your neighbor is not only found in the New Testament; It is also found in the Old Testament (Lev 19:18). Notably, there is some dispute over what the term 'neighbor' means in these texts as well. The anthropologist John Hartung argues that in the Old Testament, a 'neighbor' was thought of as one's kin rather than an outsider.[11] Hartung elaborates:

> [W]hen the Israelites received the love law, they
> were isolated in a desert. According to the account,
> they lived in tents clustered by extended families,
> they had no non-Israelite neighbors, and dissension
> was rife. Internecine fighting became rather vicious,
> with about 3,000 killed in a single episode (Exodus
> 32:26-28). Most of the troops wanted to 'choose a
> [new] captain and go back to Egypt' (Numbers 14:4).
> But their old captain, Moses, preferred group cohe-
> sion. If we want to know who Moses thought his god
> meant by neighbor, the law must be put into context,
> and the minimum context that makes sense is the
> biblical verse from which the love law is so frequently
> extracted.[12]

In fact, the Rollins Professor of History Emeritus at
Princeton University, Peter Brown, says that "The teaching of
the church defined for the Chritian who was *not* his neighbor:
the neighbor of the Christian was *not* necessarily his kinsman,
not his fellow dweller in a *quartier*, *not* his compatriot or his
fellow townsman; his neighbor was his fellow Christian."[13]

But Are Secular Rights, Universal Rights?

Even if there is a dispute in Christian scholarship over what
these terms suggest, Christian apologists still do not get rid of
their inadequate theoretical framework for "universal morality," as we saw in the previous chapters on Christian morality.
Are Christians any closer to "universal" human rights?

The philosophical and argumentative appeal to divine
revelation is tough to universalize, and Christians have no way
to ignore this dilemma. An argument that relies on divine revelation simply states that an opinion is right because "my sacred book says it is." Unfortunately, engaging with those who
argue for these views is as futile as the argument itself since
there is no way to persuade someone of its falsity. It is, by defin-

ition, unfalsifiable.

Furthermore, Christians have the more pressing question of how they will universalize a morality that is not inclusive to minorities, whether that is to the LGBTQ+ community, or even to atheists and others that according to them "infringe" on their freedoms for wanting more separation between church and state. The inclusive umbrella of Christianity extends only so far, critics say. Susan Jacoby explains:

> We can answer the question of what the Western world would have been like without the Enlightenment because we can see what other human beings are enduring now for holding the wrong beliefs in the wrong place at the wrong time, in societies where so-called secular law is subordinate to the laws and lawlessness of self-appointed spokesmen for God.[14]

Persecuted or Persecutor?

It is often said that early Christians had it bad under pagan rule. We hear stories of Christians being crucified, sent to the Colosseum to be eaten by lions, or killed by gladiators in reenacted battle scenes of Roman victories. Both Hollywood and Christian thinkers had popularized the idea that Christians were particularly persecuted before Christianity was adopted as the Roman Empire's main religion.

There were indeed cases of injustice from the pagans early on, such as with Emperor Nero. But these seem to be exceptions from the rest and the much harsher and greater persecutions that Christians inflicted on other Christians, Jews, and Muslims. In one occurrence between the Catholics and Protestants, the St Bartholomew's Day Massacre, between 5,000 to 10,000 Protestants, were killed at the hands of Catholics in a matter of 24 hours. More Christians were killed in these 24 hours than by pagans in the Roman Empire throughout its entire existence.[15]

Jews were repeatedly targeted throughout Christendom, which may be one of Christianity's most significant faults. Tertullian, one of the founders of Western theology, was particularly vitriolic toward the Jews. Tertullian went so far to argue that the vast amount of commandments in the Torah were to prevent Jews from their tendency for idolatry, sensuality, and greed.[16] In fact, throughout most of Christendom, Christians were prejudiced against Jews because they believed that Jews were ultimately to blame for their Messiah's death. In 1301 at Valencia, 11,000 Jews were forced to baptize at the price of death, meanwhile, in the same year, entire towns were burned, and Jewish populations killed.[17] These were not stand-alone occasions.

When Christianity was the superpower of Europe in the medieval ages, wars did not become less regular, as one would presume with Christendom's "universal morality." Peter Brecke estimates that approximately 1,148 conflicts arose between 900 CE and 1400 CE.[18] There appear to be almost two new conflicts annually for eleven hundred years.[19] Among these "moral blunders" were the Crusades, the Inquisitions, witch hunts, the Nine Years' War, the Thirty Years' War, the Eighty Years' War, the French Wars of Religion, the Wars of the Three Kingdoms, and the English Civil War, to name a few.[20]

When it comes to the Crusades alone, Rummel estimates that between 1095 and 1208, Crusader armies killed up to 1 million people on their way to retake Jerusalem, massacring Nicea, Antioch, and Constantinople.[21] To put that into perspective, the world had about 400 million inhabitants at the time, meaning that the death toll in proportion to the world population today would be close to 6 million, similar to the death toll of Jews in the Nazi Holocaust.[22]

Needless to say, there were many different reasons for these wars; Religion cannot be solely to blame. Nonetheless, Christianity featured several influential voices that thought that persecution and forced conversion were not only justifiable but necessary. And this certainly influenced Christendom.

Conversion

In her book, *Strange Gods: A Secular History of Conversion,* Jacoby helpfully traces the story of conversion seen in Christendom from its genesis in Jerusalem and the Peloponnesus to its steady downfall in France and England during the Enlightenment. She writes that the Christian conviction in early Christendom was that rejecting God was a "moral error of the highest order," which meant that it was the "right and duty of the state to enforce one faith."[23]

Augustine was an outright proponent of this view. Other Church notables, including Ambrose, Leo, and Martin of Tours, argued that executing heretics was a harsh admonishment; Instead, they thought it would be wiser to simply condemn them.[24] Despite the advocacy for milder treatment, the execution of heretics was common-place by the 10th century.

In John Calvin's Geneva, citizens were forbidden gambling, playing cards, dancing, fornication, witchcraft, and reading books that were not given an imprimatur by the legal enforcement agency, called the Consistory.[25] Therefore, prisons in Geneva were often full. Geneva's legal force also regulated the amount of meat that could be eaten with each meal, restricted family gatherings that exceeded 20 people, prohibited eating pastries and candied fruits, the skipping of sermons, and the naming of children after Roman-Catholic saints.[26] Jacoby goes so far to call Calvin the "most intolerant of the major founders of the Reformation."[27]

Hatred directed toward ethnic groups, among other minorities, was common among influential Church leaders. When it came to Jews, Calvin wrote:

> Some say that because the crime consists only of words there is no cause for such severe punishment. But we muzzle dogs; shall we leave men free to open their mouth and say what they please? . . . God makes it plain that the false prophet is to be stoned with-

out mercy. We are to crush beneath our heels all natural affection when his honour is at stake. The father
should not spare his child, nor the husband, his wife,
nor the friend that friend who is dearer to him than
life..[28]

Historical Christianity was not particularly inclusive,
nor did it stress liberty, freedom, and the pursuit of happiness
as many American Christians do today. In fact, each of the great
fathers of Protestantism, including Zwingli, Calvin, and Luther,
were "hostile" to freedom of conscience.[29] Luther was similarly
adamant and vitriolic toward the Jews as Calvin was. In his treatise, *On the Jews and Their Lies*, Luther writes:

First, ... set fire to their synagogues or schools and ...
bury and cover with dirt whatever will not burn, so
that no man will ever again see a stone or cinder of
them. .... Second, I advise that their houses also be
razed and destroyed. .... Third, I advise that all their
prayer books and Talmudic writings, in which such
idolatry, lies, cursing, and blasphemy are taught, be
taken from them. ..... Fourth, I advise that their rabbis
be forbidden to teach henceforth on pain of loss of
life and limb. .... Fifth, I advise that safe-conduct on
the highways be abolished completely for the Jews. ...
Sixth, I advise that usury be prohibited to them, and
that all cash and treasure of silver and gold be taken
from them and put aside for safekeeping. Seventh, I
recommend putting a flail, an ax, a hoe, a spade, a dis-
taff, or a spindle into the hands of young, strong Jews
and Jewesses and letting them earn their bread in the
sweat of their brow, as was imposed on the children of
Adam.[30]

There was some opposition to the Reformation leaders,
and indeed, Luther had at one point said that executing heretics was something that the Holy Spirit would not be pleased

with.[31] The contemporary of Calvin, Sebastian Castellio, wrote in *Concerning Heretics, Whether they are to be Persecuted*, that Calvin and other Protestants should differentiate between essential and inessential Christian doctrine to discern who is worth executing. For example, Castellio considered the doctrines of predestination, the Trinity, and the nature of heaven and hell, inessential views that one should not be killed for.[32] In his writings, Castellio was referring primarily to Servetus's execution by Calvin for denying the Trinity and rejecting infant baptism.[33] Notably, these executions were becoming less prevalent because of the writings of Christian thinkers, such as Castellio.

Atheists were also persecuted; However, they were not as common in Europe. Atheists, such as Cesare Vanini, who died at the stake in 1619, were still being executed in Europe by having their tongues pulled out and then burned alive up until the 17th century. It was not until the end of the eighteenth century that Christians stopped having stiff legal penalties in Britain for "impiety." In 1763, 70-year old Peter Annet was sentenced to a year of hard labor for questioning the accounts of miracles in the Old Testament.[34] However, it should be pointed out that 17th century Europe was far from 15th century Europe when it came to what discussions were off-limits and what type of behavior was permitted in European society.[35]

The writings of John Locke in the 17th century helped with the tolerance that was increasingly seen in Europe, especially in England. Locke could not spare his tolerance for atheists, however.[36] For example, he refused to engage with the philosopher Thomas Hobbes because Hobbes identified as an atheist. When it came to religious affiliation, Locke was more progressive than he was with regard to atheists. Locke, himself a Christian, although there is some debate over whether he had a more deistic view of God, thought that conversion should be voluntary. In Locke's words:

> A Church, then, I take to be a voluntary society of
> men, joining themselves together of their own ac-

cord, in order for the public worshipping of God, in such a manner as they judge acceptable to him, and effectual to the salvation of their souls. I say it is a free and voluntary society. Nobody is born a member of any Church; otherwise the religion of the parents would descend unto the children, by the same right of inheritance as their temporal estates, and everyone would hold his faith by the same tenure as he holds his lands; than which nothing can be imagined more absurd.[37]

Many philosophers in the 17th and 18th centuries adopted similar views. Meanwhile, Protestant and Catholic thinkers up to the 17th century thought of religious intolerance as a prerequisite to sharing their faith.[38] Although, there were rare glimpses of hope even from the most vitriolic anti-semites of the Reformation. In *That Jesus Christ was a Born Jew*, Luther writes:

If we wish to make them better, we must deal with them not according to the law of the pope, but according to the law of Christian charity. We must receive them kindly, and follow them to compete with us in earning a livelihood, so that they may have a good reason to be with us and among us and an opportunity to witness Christian life and doctrine; and if some remain obstinate, what of it? Not every one of us is a good Christian.[39]

However, as William Nichols points out in *Christian Anti-semitism: A History of Hate*, even this "humane" and "charitable" take on Jews from Luther was principally about making the Jews "better"; Nichols explains that, "Luther does not attempt to comprehend or evaluate positively the Judaism by which they live."[40] Luther very well may have been a product of his culture, but the question then is where our "universal" human rights and values came from if we cannot see them from the major Church founders.

Jews were finally given legal equality in the 1790s in the West, beginning with the United States, France, and the Netherlands, with the rest of Europe following suit in the following century.[41] It should be pointed out, however, that the Calvinistic Netherlands improved the relations between Christians and Jews "well before" that of France and Germany where the Enlightenment was in full effect.[42] Some places saw the utility of pluralism and tolerance when it came to different faiths. Nichols comments that the Reformation may have led to more religious pluralism in society, but it was by no means a purposeful move by the Reformers: "The Reformation was not therefore the precursor of modern liberalism but (in the areas it influenced) the last kick of the medieval world."[43]

Atheists, on the other hand, were still not allowed university positions well into the 20th century. Of course, it was not until recently that other minorities in many developed countries were given legal rights to rightfully participate in democracy.

Early Modern Europe

The freedom some of us experience today is, therefore, a complete novelty. Five hundred years ago, education, wealth, voting, and the freedom to travel were all reserved to aristocrats and senior clergy.[44] Around the 1500s, Europe saw drastic change. Europe's population increased from sixty-nine million in 1500 to eighty-nine million in the year 1600, almost by 30 percent.[45] With that increase in population, Europe also saw a rise in trade, freedom, diversity, and political order. Between 1470 and the early 19th century, the Western European merchant fleet grew seventeenfold.[46] Francis Fukuyama explains this growth in Europe in *The Origins of Political Order*, "[T]he early development of European states was rooted in their ability to provide justice."[47]

From the sixteenth century onwards, increasing tax rates were rooted in the need to finance war, expand, and provide more economic fortune.[48] In other words, states in Europe in the early modern period exchanged some legal rights to citizens in exchange for monetary funds to finance wars. Ninety percent of the Dutch Republic's budget was spent on war when facing off the Spanish king; similarly, 98 percent of the Habsburg Empire's budget financed its wars with Turkey and Protestants in the seventeenth century.[49]

In the 1500s in Europe, the reduction of dialects in states for one that was used at court, along with homogenized social customs, and common legal and commercial standards, made trade easier, allowing for unprecedented growth in cooperation and subsequently wealth.[50] Most importantly, the concept of the individual was harnessed beginning in the 15th and 16th centuries, gaining traction in some societies sooner than others.

England, for example, was the first to adopt liberties concerning freedom of conscience in Europe. It took some time until the most considerable social advancements were made, however. In 1783, public hangings became illegal; in 1834, the displaying of corpses on gibbets similarly came to an end; and by 1861, the number of capital offenses in England was reduced from 222 to 4.[51] These progressive shifts in England, brought prominent continental philosophers such as the French philosopher Voltaire to look at Englishmen with envy.

Most Enlightenment *philosophes* were well aware that in 18th century continental Europe, the words uttered on pen and paper could still send you to prison.[52] In 1733, Voltaire wrote: "The English are the only nation on earth who have been able to prescribe limits to the power of Kings by resisting them, and by a series of struggles have established that wise government where the Prince is all-powerful to do good, and the same time is restrained from committing evil; where the nobles are great without insolence, though there are no vassals; and where the people share in the government without confusion."[53] England became the place to be in Europe, at least until greater freedoms were ensured elsewhere.

A Brief History of Human Rights

The genesis of human rights can be traced further back, notably. Human rights are thought to have originated from the West, but similar philosophical principles can also be found in Confucian, Hindu, and Buddhist traditions.[54] The protection of human freedom and a sense of dignity can be traced as far back to Hammurabi's Code in Babylon (approximately 1780 BCE). Although, human rights as we know them today can more closely be traced from (1) the *Magna Carta* of 1215, a contract between King John and the Barons who were against the harsh taxes admonished by the monarchy, and (2) the *English Bill of Rights* of 1689.[55]

The work that followed, primarily that of Locke and Jean-Jacques Rousseau were among the more influential. Locke's *Second Treatise of Government* (1690) called for the government to uphold the "natural rights" of legal citizens in the form of a social contract between them and the state. In the 'state of nature,' each citizen was in 'a state of liberty.' Locke thought it was immoral to abuse the liberty of citizens by imposing on their natural rights because it would violate what he thought of as their natural right. Rousseau in *The Social Contract* (1762) argued that citizens should be allowed to have private interests that conflict with the people's common interests. In fact, the crux of Rousseau's work was in that he sought to find a way for human freedom to flourish despite our increasing dependency on one another.[56]

The 18th century was eventful when it came to the writings of philosophers and the texts that ensued in Constitutions across the Globe. Locke's writing markedly influenced both the American *Declaration of Independence* and its French counterpart. In 1776, the American *Declaration of Independence* claimed: "We hold these truths to be self-evident, that all men are created equal; that they are endowed by their Creator with certain unalienable rights; that among these are life, liberty and the pursuit of happiness." In 1789, the French *Declaration of the*

Rights of Man and of the Citizen proclaimed that "Men are born and remain free and equal in rights" and "The aim of every political association is the preservation of the natural and inalienable rights of man; these rights are liberty, property, security, and resistance to oppression."

Needless to say, these rights only applied to a specific part of the population, excluding ethnic minorities and women. There were some attempts made by women during the 18th century for being treated equally, such as in *A Vindication of the Rights of Women* by Mary Wollstonecraft Godwin (1792). However, these attempts were far from accepted by the mainstream and sadly fell on deaf ears.

One century before these declarations, Hooke, Boyle, Wren, Descartes, Kepler, Pascal, Leibniz, Hobbes, Spinoza, and Locke all paved the way for these Declarations, using empirical principles which slowly replaced the "divine rights of kings" and "the doctrines of theology."[57] They thus set the stage for a more nuanced view of state affairs, where theology had less of a bearing on the lives of citizens. The 18th century applied these same empirical principles to politics, society, education, law, and human rights.[58]

Many that followed disagreed with some of Locke's propositions despite how influential they were on the rights and freedoms of legal citizens. David Hume, for example, thought that Locke's justification of monarch rule was ill-advised and that it would be entirely just to rebel against absolutist monarchs. In Hume's *Of the Original Contract*, Hume adamantly expressed that "absolute monarchy is inconsistent with civil society."[59] Jeremy Bentham disagreed with Locke on natural rights, claiming that they were merely theoretical and instead called for "real" legal rights. Bentham went so far as to say that the notion that "All men are born free" is "Absurd and miserable nonsense."[60] Bentham, along with his utilitarian successor, John Stuart Mill, argued for a social utilitarian theory in politics which one could say originated with Aristotle himself, where maximizing happiness in society is seen as the highest value.

Since then, the literature on human rights has become somewhat more tedious and analytical. It remains in the ivory towers of academia with John Rawl's work, *A Theory of Justice* and Alan Gewirth's, *Reason and Morality*. Rawls, among the most influential political philosophers of the 20th century, attempted to replace the reasoning of Locke, Rousseau, and Kant with "more rational" principles.[61] For Rawls, this humble task would be accomplished by effectively arguing that justice is a matter of fairness. To argue for justice as fairness, he claimed that we must imagine an 'original position' and a 'veil of ignorance.' In doing so, we would be able to see clearly and dispose of our inherent biases, he argued. Rawls' arguments and the reactions to them by other political philosophers such as Thomas Nagel and Robert Nozick are among the last contributions to the philosophy on human rights.

When theorists discuss human rights, it can be disheartening because they use complicated language to defend positions that should be self-explanatory. I firmly believe that we should not be forced to knock on the doors of academia to discuss these topics, where reason and morality sit in the company of these intellectuals. Instead, it must be possible to justify having human rights without fully understanding the philosophy behind them. In other words, I believe that a stance on human rights is justifiable despite not being able to know how or why. As I stated before, most citizens living everyday lives simply have no time to debate the declarations made by politicians and political philosophers.

Our human rights exist in an arbitrary space, one that relies on tacit consent. This view has a place even in the halls of academia, surprisingly. Richard Rorty, for example, argues that our growth in appreciation for human rights has a lot to do with "sad and sentimental stories" rather than "increased moral knowledge."[62] The American lawyer Alan Dershowitz, who has recently come under public scrutiny for his relationship with sex offender Jeffrey Epstein, has similarly argued that human rights come from our everyday experience of injustice or, in other words, "rights come from wrongs."[63] Many others have adopted similar views.

When politicians or activists refer to "human rights" today, they refer to international and national laws.[64] Among these laws, the one that stands out, the Universal Declaration of Human Rights issued by the UN General Assembly (1948), was established to guarantee legal rights to silenced voices. The International Criminal Court and other legal courts and tribunals are responsible for prosecuting human rights violations across the Globe. The question of whether this was and is effective has been discussed at length elsewhere.[65]

The Rights Revolution

Most of the rights we experience today are not in the form that we saw with the philosophical discussions of Locke, Rousseau, Hume, and others. Today, our liberties are much more expansive. They include the rights of women, sexual minorities, ethnic minorities, and many more. The years leading up to the Rights Revolution of the 1960s can show the battle of ideas that helped the inclusivity seen today. Notably, there is still much progress to be made. In 2006, there were still fifty-three countries in the world where husbands could not be prosecuted for raping their wives.[66] We can hope for more change to come and speak out against these injustices as often as we can.

We should appreciate how far we have come, however. In large part, we can thank the rights revolution in the United States. The years leading up to the rights revolution were crucial in planting fertile ground for change. The 1940s and '50s were in the words of Peter Watson, embodied by "the decline of the doctrine of original sin," where individuals were not seen as totally and inherently depraved as they were before.[67] Instead, the individual started gaining more credence. That meant that during the 1940s, feminist literature started appearing in the public sphere, including Simone de Beauvoir's monumental *The Second Sex* (1949) and *Modern Woman: The Lost Sex* (1947) by Ferdinand Lundberg and Marynia Farnham. The influence of these publications and the social movements that manifested in conjunction with them in the 1940s meant that more and more women were likely to lose their virginity before marriage, serve on juries, and attend college than at any prior point in history.[68] More importantly, women were finally being given the rights they deserved.

The era of the Rights Revolution was notably a time of sharp disagreement with Christian thinkers because of the association the Rights Revolution had with postmodernism, moral relativism, and the end of the traditional family. Michel Foucault, one of the champions of postmodernist thought, was homosexual himself and argued for the legitimization and decriminalization of same-sex relations in culture.

The conservative morality of Christians was still widely held well into the 20th century, as many will remember. Interestingly enough, same-sex relations were fairly common in Ancient Greece but were supplanted by Christian dogma that held that those that practice same-sex relations will not inherit the "kingdom of God" (1 Cor 6:9). During the Enlightenment, thinkers such as Montesquieu and Voltaire argued that same-sex relations should be decriminalized. Later, Bentham, applying utilitarian arguments, argued that homosexuality was morally acceptable since it did not harm others.[69] The widespread acceptance of homosexual individuals today in culture is by no means a Christian achievement. Granted, I do not know of anyone that would suggest this.

Some argue that women's rights are similarly vacuous within the Christian framework since they were entirely non-existent in the medieval era. Bertrand Russell says that the belief that Christianity in some way improved the status of women is one of the "grossest perversions of history."[70] As I've shown in my chapter on Christian human rights, the New Testament may feature several passages that make a case for rights, but these made little to no historical precedent. The way we read those texts today is drastically different from the way they were interpreted throughout Christendom.

Throughout history, women were mistreated by most civilizations, especially in the West, where Christianity gained a strong foothold over society. For instance, during the French and German witch hunts, which were predominantly persecutions made against women, between 60,000 and 100,000 people were executed (85 percent of which were women).[71] The Middle Ages featured some opposition to these lynchings, but these were hardly ever effective. The most change came during the Renaissance when Erasmus, Montaigne, and Hobbes voiced their opposition to the harsh and unequal treatment of women.[72] 1716 became the last year a woman was hanged in Europe and 1749 the last year a woman was burned at the stake.[73]

Despite the wrong side Christianity has been on throughout history, Christians will still take credit for the development of "Western" values. Many will point out the obvious, which is that the historical record suggests something more convoluted. Peter Singer writes that most changes in the moral landscape on issues on animal rights, abortion, euthanasia, and international aid are not "from religion" but "from [a] careful reflection on humanity and what we consider a life well lived."[74] We have good reason to presume so, especially because both Eastern philosophy and other early Western philosophy stressed harmonious living well before Jesus did. The Christian tendency to take credit for advancements that are clearly not solely of their own volition is what led Michael Shermer to conclude:

> I predict that within a few years, maybe a decade, white Christians will come around to treating gay men and lesbians no differently from how they now treat other groups whom they previously persecuted - women, Jews, blacks. These changes will not occur because of some new interpretation of a biblical passage or because of a new revelation from God. These changes will come about the same way they do: by the oppressed minority fighting for the right to be treated

equally, and by enlightened members of the oppress-
ing majority supporting their cause. Then Christian
churches will take credit for the civil liberation of
the gay community, rummage through the historical
record and find those preachers who had the courage
and the character to stand up for gay rights when their
fellow Christians would not, and then cite those as
evidence that, were it not for Christianity, gay people
would still be in the closet.[75]

What Caused the Rights Revolution?

As for what caused the Rights Revolution of the 1960s in America, there is no way to know for sure, but some have speculated.
Christians will love to take credit for it all, as Shermer points
out. But I believe there are better theories. One, for example,
could be the invention of the Printing Press.

Pinker explains that "advances in publishing" led to an
increase of books and literacy, resulting in the "popularity of
the novel" in the 18th century.[76] He argues that this may have
given moral insight into the life of social classes that were
largely ignored and allowed for empathy that was not there before that point. In this way, Mark Twain in writing *Adventures of
Huckleberry Finn* and Harriet Beecher Stowe in *Uncle Tom's Cabin*
helped raise awareness for the humanity of African-American
slaves; Charles Dickens' *Oliver Twist* (1838) and *Nicholas Nickleby*
(1839) gave insight into the lives of children in orphanages, and
so forth.[77] Pinker concludes, "[T]he explosion of reading may
have contributed to the Humanitarian Revolution by getting
people into the habit of straying from their parochial vantage
points."[78] This idea was also advanced by the historian Lynn
Hunt and psychologists Raymond Mar and Keith Oatley.[79] Although there is only little evidence that can confirm this theory.

Another possibility is that humanitarian movements originated from urbanized environments where philosophers and
revolutionaries spent most of their living moments. London,

Paris, and Amsterdam, Pinker explains, were "intellectual bazaars" where thinkers discussed philosophy among each other in coffeehouses, bookstores, and salons.[80] Athens, Venice, Boston, and Philadelphia are known today as cities where democracy has its origin.[81] That can be a coincidence, of course, but it is one worth mentioning. However, this speculation is almost certainly more plausible than the claim that present-day values stem from so-called Judeo-Christian values. Such claims disregard any careful reading of history. As Kenan Malik writes in *The Quest for a Moral Compass*, "There are no historically transcendent civilizational values. What today we describe as 'Western' values would leave Aquinas and Dante bewildered, and even more so Augustine and Plato."[82]

It will be interesting to see what the 21st century has in store concerning the development of human rights. With the killing of George Floyd in 2020, for example, by the American police officer, Derek Chauvin, we saw that social media formed a social rights coalition across most of the West that called for the end to police brutality and as a result saw impressive changes on the institutional level. The city of Minneapolis, for instance, disbanded its entire police departments in response to protests. Other counties and states seek to "defund" or more accurately "refund" police budgets into different, more effective, ways to deal with everyday nonessential police calls. As with the moral impacts on society by the novel, we may see similar moral shifts today with the effects of social media and the ability to share disturbing video footage that rightfully provokes moral outrage in us.

Chapter 7

Christians,

Animal Rights, &
Climate Change

I praise you, for I am fearfully and wonderfully made. Ps 139:14

Secular man may say he cares for the tree because if he cuts it down, his cities will not be able to breathe. But that is egoism, and egoism will produce ugliness, no matter how long it takes or what fine words are used. – Francis Schaeffer[1]

Climate change is a concern for future generations, not for today, critics say. But the numbers are pointing to something else. In 2017, climate change cost the United States $306 billion, writes David Wallace-Wells in his frightening but important book, *The Uninhabitable Earth: Life After Warming.*[2] If the world continues under "business-as-usual" conditions, he explains, we will continue to experience a loss of $551 trillion in damages at 3.7 degrees warming by 2100.[3] And according to the United Nations, we are headed that direction inevitably. In fact, experts warn that we are expected to hit 4.5 degrees warming by 2100.[4]

As of today, pollution is already killing as many as nine million people annually.[5] By 2050, it is estimated that sub-Saharan Africa, South Asia, and Latin America will generate more than 140 million climate refugees, as I touched on in my previous chapter.[6] Other major cities will also be evacuated, including Miami, New Jersey, Hong Kong, Baghdad, Paris, New York, Montreal, Seattle, creating countless more refugees. The problem is that large portions of the population live within thirty feet of sea level, 600 million people to be precise, and these areas are expected to be hit the most.[7]

One of the most recent reports from The United Nations' Intergovernmental Panel on Climate Change (IPCC) says that even if everyone stops polluting all at once, we'll still get to 3.2-degree warming. 3.2-degree warming would mean that 100 urban centers would be flooded, including Miami, Dhaka, Shanghai, Hong Kong, New York, Montreal, Seattle, London, Baghdad, San Francisco, Sacramento, Houston, Philadelphia, Florida (97%), and 70% of New Jersey. The trend toward increased flooding is escalating. From 1992 to 1997, 49 billion tons of ice of the Antarctic ice sheet melted annually on average. From 2012 to 2017, that number increased to 219 billion tons of ice melting annually. Since the 1950s, the Antarctic has lost 13,000 square miles from its ice shelf. Experts suggest that the fate of it will be determined by the action taken within the next decade.[8]

In fact, 2.4 million American homes and businesses — $1 trillion in value — are expected to experience chronic flooding.[9] Ninety-seven percent of Florida will be off the map by 2100, argues David Archer, a leading ocean chemist.[10] The science on this is irrefutable, experts claim. The predictions may vary in severity. Business-as-usual will, however, not prevent apocalyptic calamities from regularly occurring. So, the urgency is apparent.

For atheists, life on Earth may be all there is. That is why, for them, solving man-made climate change is of high importance. If by 2100, we find ourselves in a truly "uninhabitable earth," as Wallace-Wells says we may, then we lose everything. Some estimates suggest that it is unlikely that man-made climate change will eradicate our species. But near extinction is enough reason to act. The question is whether Christians can be urgent on climate issues. My answer to this is both yes and no because Christians have one thing that is slightly more urgent than the climate and the preservation of the species: eternity.

Biblical Climate Change Action

The Bible presents a mixed account on the responsibility of humans to preserve the earth. Wayne Grudem writes that "[T]he Bible's picture of the earth *in general* is that it has abundant resources that God has put there to bring great benefit to us as human beings made in his image. There is no hint that mankind will ever exhaust the earth's resources by developing them and using them wisely."[11] The authors of Genesis write:

> While the earth remains, seedtime and harvest, cold and heat, summer and winter, day and night, shall not cease. Genesis 8:22

> I establish my covenant with you, that never again shall all flesh be cut off by the waters of the flood, and never again shall there be a flood to destroy the earth." And God said, "This is the sign of the covenant that I make between me and you and every living creature that is with you, for all future generations: I have set my bow in the cloud, and it shall be a sign of the covenant between me and the earth. When I bring clouds over the earth and the bow is seen in the clouds, I will remember my covenant that is between me and you and every living creature of all flesh. And the waters shall never again become a flood to destroy all flesh. Genesis 9:11-15

These passages indicate that God expects His people to preserve the gifts of God. However, the Bible is also clear on the inevitable destruction of the Earth. Although these passages may be metaphorical and in no way suggest that the Bible prophesied man-made climate change in the 21st century. Some of these passages include:

> For nation will rise against nation, and kingdom against kingdom, and there will be famines and earthquakes in various places. Matthew 24:7

> There will be great earthquakes, and in various places famines and pestilences. And there will be terrors and great signs from heaven. Luke 21:11

> When the Lamb opened the seventh seal, there was silence in heaven for about half an hour. Then I saw the seven angels who stand before God, and seven trumpets were given to them. And another angel came and stood at the altar with a golden censer, and he was given much incense to offer with the prayers of all the saints on the golden altar before the throne, and the smoke of the incense, with the prayers of the saints, rose before God from the hand of the angel. Then the angel took the censer and filled it with fire from the altar and threw it on the earth, and there were peals of thunder, rumblings, flashes of lightning, and an earthquake. Revelation 8:1-13

Apart from wanting to take care of God's Creation, as God called them to, Christians do not have any other biblical reason to find solutions to man-made climate change. There is only instrumental value in nature for the Christian, value in service for different causes, not intrinsic value, value for its own sake, since nature directly proves God's existence according to the Bible (Romans 1:20). Apart from that, the Bible is not clear on why we should protect nature in the first place.

The Bible's silence on this is arguably why many in the Christian right do not prioritize man-made climate change in their sermons. In the end, eternity is on the line, and preaching the Gospel comes before taking care of the environment we live in. Needless to say, when the global concern becomes much more apparent and demanding, Christian leaders will have to be more outspoken on these issues because of their influence and the tangible ethical consequences of not speaking up. Some Christians have started to do so already.

Francis Schaeffer, one of the leading Christian thinkers of the 20th century, tackles environmentalism in his book, *Pollution and the Death of Man: The Christian View of Ecology*. Schaeffer was not your typical Christian thinker. He had hippie-like sensibilities and, upon moving to the United States in 1948, even forsook the possession of his car. Schaeffer would frequently go on hikes, tend to his garden, and regularly traveled across the world because of his love of nature. He would pick up trash from the hiking trails on his hikes with students and objected to waste being thrown overboard on his boat trips overseas.[12]

In his book, Schaeffer writes that only the Christian can unite on environmental matters because "God has spoken" on it.[13] He blames humanism and rationalism for "looking at the particulars" to then make a universal, which he believes is philosophically futile and arbitrary.[14] He blames our current environmental predicament on humanism. There's nothing new under the sun, it seems; Atheism is always to blame.

That is not to say that Christianity has the answer outright for Schaeffer, but instead that it is the most compelling worldview that provides a solution to big questions such as man-made climate change.[15] Schaeffer believes that because Creation is a gift from God, only Christians have a justified reason to care for it. Indeed, Schaeffer writes that "[Christians] treat nature with respect because God made it."[16] The question then is why so few Christians prioritize speaking about nature and protecting it if Christians are the only ones who can experience unity on this issue.

Animal Rights
Closely tied with the preservation of the Earth is the issue of

factory-farming and animal rights. As I hoped to show in my previous chapter on whether Christians do indeed have a way of defending the sanctity of human life biblically, I hope to provide a similar analysis of whether Christians have any way of defending animal rights.

Historically, animals were not given much thought as to whether they should have any rights at all. The father of modern philosophy, Rene Descartes, for example, nailed living dogs to wood, digging into them searching for a soul, which he could not find.[17] One has to wonder why this "scientific" experiment did not extend to humans.

The experiments slowly became more humane, as scientists figured out that animals have cognitive abilities and are sentient as we are. However, progress can still be made here as well. Societies across the Globe are making considerable advancements in treating animals with the dignity they deserve. These advancements were seen as early as 1800 when laws against bear beating were established in the British Parliament.[18] By 1835, The Ill-Treatment of Cattle Act extended protection to bulls, dogs, and cats.[19]

Fast-forward to the 21st century and many societies have outlawed blood sports, including foxhunts and bloodhounds in 2005, cockfights in 2008, and bullfights in 2010.[20] Society is slowly catching up with what science has been telling us for years. In fact, Dr. Nicholas Dodman, the Professor at Cummings School of Veterinary Medicine at Tufts University, claims that "With every passing year the cognitive gap that supposedly differentiates us from mere animals is shrinking."[21]

Of course, the underlying premise for Christians for defending these animals is much different than for those who are non-Christian or unbelievers. Throughout the Bible, animals are treated with indignation, often slaughtered alongside entire cities and tribes, because they made the simple mistake of being in the wrong place at the wrong time. One memorable and particularly barbaric occasion was when animals were punished alongside humans in Noah's flood. Some animals, precisely two members of each species, were spared by God. But most of them drowned along with the humans that God thought were unforgivable enough to kill. The question in that story is why God had to drown seemingly innocent animals for crimes that were not their own. If animals had nothing to do with the sinful condition of humans, then why would God need to punish them? Because of our understanding of animal sentience today, the killing of these animals is even more barbaric.

Many Christians will justify treating animals decently based on Christian teaching to take care of God's creation, but they do not go as far as the science tells us to. In fact, many Christian thinkers have voiced concerns about focusing too much on the rights of animals because of what they insist that will do to the value of human life.

In *A Rat Is a Pig Is a Dog Is a Boy: The Human Cost of the Animal Rights Movement*, Wesley J. Smith writes that the animal rights movement of the 1970s was an "antihuman ideology."[22] Smith is persuaded that 'Human exceptionalism,' that humans are a particularly unique species, is the only basis for universal human rights. And that since the animal rights movement rejects this premise, it is actively harming our well-being. Smith does not call for altogether abandoning suffering animals, however, and argues that the "core obligation of human exceptionalism" is never to cause animals suffering for "frivolous reasons."[23] Smith continues that we cannot define rights "Without the conviction that humankind has unique worth based on our nature rather than our individual capacities."[24] Without human exceptionalism, Smith firmly believes, "[U]niversal human rights are impossible to sustain philosophically."[25]

Nicholas Christakis disagrees with Smith's belief that exposing the similarities between animals and humans rids us of a meaningful basis for human rights. In the words of Christakis, "[W]hen we resemble other animals with respect to the social suite, it binds us all together. The more like these animals we are, the more alike we humans must be to one another."[26] In his book, *Blueprint*, Christakis writes that it is a fictitious notion to think of ourselves as exempt from the rest of nature. The similarities are striking, whether that is seen in the friendships of elephants, the cooperation of dolphins, and the culture of chimpanzees.[27]

Human Exceptionalism and Loving Your Neighbor

The concept of human exceptionalism is mainly a remnant from Christendom's dualism, the belief that the soul is a separate eternal entity from the physical body. Animals do not really have a purpose in the Garden of Eden, before the Fall, apart from glorifying God and giving Adam a job, in particular, to name them. God creates humans in His image, meaning that we have a soul and moral conscience (Gen 1:27). The consensus of the Christian right, perhaps even of Christianity at large, on this is clear, "[H]uman beings are much more valuable in God's sight than animals."[28] The Bible starts as early as Genesis 1:28 in clarifying on how humans should treat animals:

> And God said to them, "Be fruitful and multiply and fill the earth and *subdue it*, and *have dominion over* the fish of the sea and over the birds of the heavens and over *every living thing* that moves on the earth."

In one passage in the New Testament, Jesus exorcises a Legion of demons, letting them enter into a herd of pigs, numbering at about 2,000, who then run into the Black Sea and drown (Mark 5:13). In another revealing passage in the Old Testament, Saul is asked to "strike Amalek and devote to destruction all that they have," including "man and woman, child and infant, ox and sheep, camel and donkey" (1 Samuel 15:3). Saul fails to slaughter all the Amalekites and animals, for which Saul suffered severe punishment. In what way did Saul fail his God? He kept some animals for sacrifice to God. Unfortunately, this was not favored in the eyes of God. The meat was "unclean."

Jesus says, "Of how much more value is a man than a sheep!" (Matt. 12:12) Jesus repeats this sentiment with regard to the "birds of the air" (Matt. 6:26) and sparrows (Matt. 10:31).

The Christian worldview poses no serious objections to animal subjugation apart from imposing unnecessary violence and cruelty on God's creation. But once again, the value is not in the animal or their rights but rather in the fact that God has given them as a gift to humans. The onus, then, is on the stewardship of these animals, not on any intrinsic worth or suffering inflicted on them.

As we have seen from previous chapters, Jesus says that among the two most important commandments is to "love your neighbor," which suggests that God cares for humans and thinks of humans of value. The Bible says that God "knows us" before our birth and "knits" us together in the womb, as we saw when discussing abortion (Ps 139:13-14, or Jeremiah 1:5). Paul goes so far as to say that God knew us before the foundations of the Earth (Eph 1:4). So, it may not be surprising that Christians do not focus all that much on animal rights or factory-farming. The problem is that animals should receive our attention especially because of how poorly they are treated. Human exceptionalism permits excuses and detachment from the insurmountable suffering factory-farming causes to animals. And that is unacceptable.

The Problem With Human Exceptionalism

Human exceptionalism often comes across as poor philosophy. In the end, what truly distinguishes humans from animals is a capacity for advanced language (allowing us to express our suffering better and cooperate) and cognitive skills. The closest animals to ourselves are chimpanzees. And many are starting to call for fairer treatment of chimpanzees because of their similarities to us, including the organization, The Great Ape Project, which calls for advanced rights for chimps. Critics of The Great Ape Project will say that humans and chimps differ at a fundamental level even if there are physical similarities between us.

Jonathan Mark writes in *What it means to be 98% chimpanzee: Apes, People, and Their Genes*, "Apes deserve protection, even rights, but not human rights."[29] For Mark, "Humans have human rights by virtue of having been born human"[30] This birth comes with the rights of citizenship, "an endowment by the state."[31] Mark further writes, "[T]he phrase 'human rights' has no meaning if it does not apply to all humans and only to humans."[32]

It is often argued in defense of chimpanzee rights, that our DNA and bone structure closely resembles chimpanzees, and we should therefore extend human rights to them. However, Marks clarifies that saying that we are 98% chimpanzee does not say much about the similarity between humans and chimps. It is true, he writes, that chimps and humans have similar bone structures, which should be of more significance he writes than DNA similarity.[33] "Genetics appropriates that discovery as a triumph because it can place a number on it, but the number is rather unreliable as such. And whatever the number is, it shouldn't be any more impressive than the anatomical similarity."[34] However, it is not for genetic reasons that we think that chimpanzees should be treated equally, as I argued above; It is instead because they can suffer.

Obviously, no one is arguing that chimps have the same rights as humans do regarding the justice system and penal code. For example, you cannot expect a chimp to be given a lawyer if accused of third-rate homicide. Mark's argument here is rather silly. Few are arguing that chimps will be given equal rights to humans. Rather, animal rights activists argue that chimps will be given the right not to be tortured needlessly in science experiments and so forth.

I don't see exactly how we are incapable of defending human rights by acknowledging that most animals are equally able to process pain and should be treated accordingly. Science has indeed revealed that almost every animal alive can suffer to a certain extent. It then follows that we should adjust our relationship with non-human animals. Otherwise, we are causing unnecessary suffering to countless sentient creatures.

The Christian will have difficulty arguing otherwise, except by applying the sort of poor philosophy that Smith and those that echo him exhibit. Shanor and Kanwal write in *Bats*

Sing, Mice Giggle that "It's well documented" that animals sing, babble, giggle, and communicate with unique dialects.[35] Mustached bats, they write, exemplify a capacity for "a vocabulary that at a phonetic level is comparable to ours"[36] In a Northern Arizona University study, prairie dogs are shown to have different accents based on which colony they are found in.[37]

Nancy F. Castaldo writes in *Beastly Brains: Exploring How Animals Think, Talk, and Feel*, that "animals utilize vocabulary, grammar, accents, and gestures." They also "communicate with vision, smell, touch, or taste as well as sounds."[38] Elephants have shown to care for injured humans, for example, and will assist members of other species that are under predatory threat.[39] Elephants have also been seen to put branches and vegetation on corpses in respect and acknowledgment of their passing.[40] They also pause in locations where one of their kind has passed for several minutes at a time, as if in memory of the deceased.[41] Frankly, the scientific consensus on this is telling. Christakis explains:

> Dogs and even rats have empathy. Crows, crocodiles, and wasps use tools. Gorillas use language. Chimpanzees and elephants form friendships. These abilities are not precisely the same as ours, but they still amaze and trouble us as we sense our continuity with the animal kingdom in fuller ways. The recognition of this continuity makes it increasingly hard, morally, to ignore that animals' muscles, which we eat, are guided by their brains, which have thoughts and feelings. As we break down barriers between ourselves and the animal world, the human claims to superiority and dominion, not just distinctiveness, break down.[42]

Human Exceptionalism and Consciousness

Even if we see similar social lives in animals, Christians will claim that we are "exceptional" as a species because of our unique capacity for consciousness. One common objection to atheism from Christian thinkers is that we have no explanation for why material (the body) resulted in something immaterial (consciousness). In philosophy, this is known as the "hard problem of consciousness." And, yes, this is a "problem" because, well, no one seems to have any answers.

Philosophers, cognitive psychologists, and neuroscientists have yet to find a compelling way to explain why consciousness arises from material beings. Christians say that they have the upper hand here, by imposing the "God of the Gaps" argument, namely that since we do not know, the explanation must be God. Needless to say, that is not a good enough reason to believe in God's existence, let alone provide a sufficient explanation for such an interesting scientific and philosophical question such as the origin of consciousness.

The philosopher Thomas Nagel is perhaps most known in philosophy for his contribution to the discussion of consciousness. In an influential paper titled "What Is It Like to Be a Bat?" Nagel argues that since we can picture what it is like to be a bat, it must follow that animals have some essence. In his own words, "An organism is conscious if there is something that it is like to be that organism."[43] However, what was previously thought to be a unique "problem" for humans, is turning out to not be so unique.

In fact, scientists say that even non-human animals have the "neuroanatomical, neurochemical, and neurophysiological substrates of conscious states along with the capacity to exhibit intentional behaviors."[44] This is significant because it would question one of the central underlying premises of human exceptionalism, namely that humans are unique in having consciousness. In 2012, world-leading neuroscientists addressed the growing research on animal consciousness in the *Cambridge Declaration on Consciousness* and concluded that "[T]he weight of evidence indicates that humans are not unique in possessing the neurological substrates that generate consciousness."[45]

We can expect further advancements in the science on

this, however. Our similarities will likely be exposed, which will make it even more challenging to justify indignance toward the suffering of animals.

Factory-Farming

It is nearly impossible to deny that factory-farming is indeed linked with man-made climate change and that it is one of the most grueling practices of our generation. It may just be remembered by future generations as one of the most abominable practices of our times, as was slavery at the height of colonialism. The United Nations estimates that if we do not change our meat-eating practices by 2050, we will need twice as much food as we do today.[46] By not changing our ways, we are certainly not helping ourselves.

Yuval Noah Harari calls factory-farming the "worst crime in history."[47] It's not hard to see why Harari would make such a bold assertion. Behind-the-scenes video footage seen in popular documentaries such as *Cowspiracy* (2014) reveal unimaginable conditions for animals. In 2009, the activist group *Mercy for Animals* showed highly controversial undercover video footage of baby-chicks being ground up alive in Iowa. Cows and hogs are often killed prematurely due to the health ramifications of staying in factory-farms. The list goes on. Videos and documentaries are disturbing the public bi-weekly with the atrocities animals in factory-farms face.

It is no secret by now that animals found in factory-farms live in disturbingly small cages, are brutally treated, and slaughtered with disregard. It is then troubling that most of the meat we consume is from factory farms. Data from the USDA Census of Agriculture and EPA definitions of Concentrated Animal Feeding Operations estimate that about 99 percent of U.S. farmed animals live in factory farms (last updated April 11, 2019). Globally, more than 200 million land animals are killed for food every day, which is around 72 billion per year.[48] Although that number may increase when China, with its 1.4 billion inhabitants, steadily enters the middle-class, suggesting that their meat-intake may change accordingly.

It is not only that factory-farming is ethically question-able, but it is also very bad for us. One study revealed that about 80% of antibiotics ever made go directly into the animals we eat.[49] The U.S. bestselling author, doctor, and assistant professor of medicine at Weill Cornell, Matt MacCarthy, explains in his book, *Superbugs: The Race to Stop an Epidemic*, that "The indiscriminate use of antibiotics in animals has been one of the primary drivers of superbugs."[50] The problem is that when bacteria are exposed to antibiotics, our "best drugs," they eventually learn how to avoid them.[51] Unfortunately, that is just how evolution works. Organisms either adapt or go extinct.

Pandemics have repeatedly been traced back to the poor conditions of factory farms and wet markets, whether that is H1N1, the swine flu, or H5N1, the bird flu, or SARS-CoV-2, more commonly known as the "Coronavirus." Indeed, the link between factory-farming and pandemics is scientifically well established.[52] Of course, the most recent of which, the Coronavirus, is not the deadliest that we can expect to come from these poor conditions. What can we do to prevent further pandemics from emerging? Well, for one, we can seriously reduce our meat-intake. There are plenty of alternatives to factory-farming. Scientists, nutritionists, and investors are developing new ways to consume the appropriate amount of nutrients to live healthy and stable lifestyles.[53] We would do well to consider them.

Eating Animals in the Bible

Despite the science on this, the Bible never condemns the eating of animals. In fact, the Bible says that "every moving thing that lives shall be food for you" (Gen 9:3). God then devotes seven chapters in Leviticus to how animals should be killed for sacrifice. Jesus himself helps the disciples fish and eats fish along with them (John 21:4-13). The question is whether a vegetarian diet at the time was at all sustainable, and according to sources, it could have been. Indeed, meat for most of history was a rarity, one that only affluent households would be able to afford. This is why we can reliably speculate, for example, that Martin Luther was from a wealthy family since thousands of pig bones were found close to his family home where Luther was raised.[54]

The Christian position toward eating meat, Grudem writes, is clear: "A Christian worldview... will present no moral objection to eating meat from various animals or to wearing leather or fur made from animal skins."[55] "Humans," in the Christian worldview, Harari explains, are the "apex of creation," while every other creature is largely ignored.[56] Where Christianity may excel biblically in terms of supplying human rights, not historically, it to an equal extent falls short at providing animals the rights they deserve.

Even if you accept the Christian worldview, you will have a difficult time defending the ethical importance of ending factory-farming and prioritizing climate change action. The countless biblical examples of God's indignance toward the suffering animals make that very clear. Yes, you are called to be a steward of God's gifts, but only for their instrumental value, rather than for their intrinsic value. I will show how the atheist may find it more worthwhile to defend our planet's future and make the lives of sentient creatures a priority in the next chapter.

Chapter 8

Atheists, Animal Rights, & Climate Change

> The notion that human life is sacred just because it is human life is medieval. –Peter Singer (Unknown source)

It was not until recently that the animal rights movement took mainstream precedence. Many consider the philosopher, Peter Singer, to have sparked the movement with his monumental book, *Animal Liberation*. Since then, PETA (People for the Ethical Treatment of Animals) and other animal rights activist movements have reached mainstream news because of their, at times, controversial activism. PETA, for one, compared the Nazi Holocaust to factory-farming today. Many took issue with this because of the apparent unempathetic ring it has to it and its inefficiency to persuade those who do not sympathize with the animal rights movement. Jacy Reese, for example, lays out a compelling case for activism that would gain more traction with moderates in society in his book, *The End of Factory Farming*. Many others believe that less intense and careful activism can do more good than the extremism seen in some animal rights organizations.

When it comes to the way atheists treat animals, there are, in fact, many good reasons not to treat them harshly. Indeed, it seems that the underlying premise of humanism can and must extend to other sentient animals. Similar arguments against treating animals harshly can be applied to how we treat the environment. For example, eliminating or severely decreasing the number of animals we eat can not only benefit animals in that it reduces suffering but it also inevitably reduces greenhouse gas emissions and decreases the probability of another pandemic outbreak from factory-farms which can harm countless more.[1]

Climate Change & Future Generations

I did not address the science on the validity of man-made climate change in the previous chapter, mainly because I do not consider myself a noteworthy authority. At times, it is good to agree with those who know much more about this than we do. And the experts do, in fact, agree. According to the Intergovernmental Panel on Climate Change, a UN-backed panel composed of thousands of climate scientists, "[I]t is extremely likely that human influence has been the dominant cause of the observed warming since the mid-twentieth century."[2] They report that the probability is at least 95 percent. One meta-analysis that reviewed four thousand academic papers found that "97.1 percent endorsed the consensus position that humans are causing global warming."[3]

Most issues that we consider as common-day knowledge falls under similar likely-to-be-true characteristics. And many things that we accept as true have very little scientific support for them, such as Christ's divinity, for example. On an individual level, many of us accept things without knowing the evidence for it because we simply do not have time or the intellectual resources to differentiate between real scientific knowledge and fake conspiracy claims. Even if man-made climate change is a myth or not scientifically verified as critics will propagate, being wrong far outweighs the cost of being right, both in financial cost and in the cost to lives. William MacAskill, writes, "[T]he mere fact that man-made climate change *might* be happening is enough to warrant action."[4] If we are wrong, it may cost us millions of lives, and the world economy will inevitably take a hit as well.

David Wallace-Wells explains that the financial cost "costs a temperate country like the United States about one percentage point of GDP" and that the world would at 1.5 degrees "be $20 trillion richer than at 2 degrees."[5] If we do take action, the costs will be much lower. MacAskill writes, "We would have wasted some amount of resources developing low-carbon technology and slowed economic progress a bit, but it wouldn't, literally, be the end of the world."[6]

These costs will soon cripple the potential of humanity. Today, more than 10,000 people die each day globally, from small-particulate pollution coming from burning carbon.[7] Annually, anywhere between 260,000 and 600,000 people die from smoke and wildfires which are linked to climate change; Indeed, "Canadian fires have been linked to spikes in hospitalizations as far away as the Eastern Seaboard of the United States."[8] We looked at some of the present-day problems with man-made climate change in the previous chapter. This is clearly not only hypothetical.

One of the most notable differences between Christian and secular (as in non-believer) views on man-made climate change and justifying renewable resources is that secular-minded citizens do not have anything to look forward to after they die. They then have some moral obligation to focus on these issues. Therefore, an argument for preserving the world is more potent since this is all there is. As we saw from the previous chapter, Christians have some reasons to care for animals and the environment, namely in that they are to be good stewards of God's creation. But it does not extend beyond that, at least not biblically.

Animals and Secular Focus

To what extent should animals be our priority in the 21st century? Singer has controversially argued that preferential treatment of humans, or "human exceptionalism," is "speciesist."

The term speciesism was originally popularized by Singer and explored the inherent bias against a sentient being because of belonging to a certain species.[9] For Singer, "[I]t would be speciesist to claim that it is *always* more seriously wrong to kill a member of the species *Homo sapiens* than it is to kill a non-human animal."[10] There are exceptions, of course.

Once again, the value of the individual in the secular view is primarily in that they are sentient, or that they can suffer. Before we discovered that consciousness and morality are not unique to humanity, or *Homo sapiens*, we thought this distinguished us from the animal kingdom. As I pointed out in my previous chapter, these characteristics are not unique to our species. Indeed, we have compelling reasons to think that both consciousness and morality have evolved separately in species that are not a part of our evolutionary lineage, suggesting that there is something about both morality and consciousness that is necessary for the effective survival of a species.

If we take this logic seriously, we have to do as Singer has and accept that treating some species as lesser simply because they are not human, is some form of discrimination, maybe even "speciesist."

How to View Ethical Dilemmas?

There are three main ethical schools in philosophy that we look at ethical dilemmas through: deontology, virtue ethics, and consequentialism (or utilitarianism). Each one of these schools of thought has its fair share of adherents. For our purposes here, I will discuss utilitarianism and show why this school of thought can guide us in treating others, including animals. Utilitarianism is an ethical school of thought that says that the most moral action is one that promotes the highest amount of good for the most number of people. Jeremy Bentham originally proposed the argument behind utilitarianism and even extended the logic to reducing the suffering of animals. Concerning the suffering of animals, Bentham writes: "The question is not Can they *reason?* nor Can they *talk?* but, Can they *suffer?*"

Kenan Malik explains that Bentham's insistence that "good and bad, right and wrong" should not be defined by revelation, intuition, or judged by motive and instead be judged by their consequences was "historically revolutionary."[11] His successor, John Stuart Mill, expanded on this idea and argued that the quality of pleasure is also important, whereas Bentham only considered the quantity.

There are many significant problems with utilitarianism, obviously. For one, it may not always be the case that the rights of sentient beings will be upheld if the highest good for the most number of people is the prime determinant of moral action. Utilitarians have thought of these problems, of course, leading them to differentiate between Act and Rule Utilitarianism, for example. However, critics have rightly pointed out that this ethical school of thought is robotic and indignant toward suffering worldwide.

Joshua Greene discusses the critics of utilitarianism in his book *Moral Tribes*. In Greene's view, there is no such thing as a coherent moral philosophy; We should never expect to come up with one. It is our choice to look at present-day ethical dilemmas through the lens of one that makes the most sense to the most people; We need a moral framework that is consistent to all beings and is not selective:

> [A]ny truly coherent philosophy is bound to offend us, sometimes in the real world but especially in the world of philosophical thought experiments, in which one can artificially pit our strongest feelings against the greater good. We've underestimated utilitarianism because we've overestimated our own minds. We've mistakenly assumed that our gut reactions are reliable guides to moral truth.[12]

Greene argues that utilitarianism is our best current bet at creating a "metamorality" for moral truth; And that with it, we can better combat the "automatic settings" that we have adopted from biology and culture.[13]

Animal Suffering

Apart from the claim that animals are not different from us on some metaphysical level or by not having what was previously thought as unique human characteristics, such as consciousness and non-kin altruism, the argument for reducing animal suffering can be defended by an emphasis on the intrinsic good of treating others well. Indeed, the argument for reducing the suffering of animals is pretty straight forward. Here is the argument in one form, highlighted by Singer in his book, *The Life You Can Save*:

1. Modern animal agriculture causes an immense amount of suffering.
2. We are responsible both for what we do and for what we refrain from doing.
3. We have the means to reduce the suffering caused by modern animal agriculture. Therefore:
4. It is imperative for each of us to do so.[14]

As I showed in the previous part of the book, the argument for eradicating factory-farming also extends to reducing gas house emissions and reducing the likelihood of another pandemic. Perhaps the only point of disagreement with an argument like this denies that we should care about the suffering that animal agriculture causes to animals. With the information readily available to anyone who has access to the internet, it seems that many do not care. If we are to think of animals as truly sentient creatures that deserve some basic form of rights, then we would do well to discard the concept of human exceptionalism.

Christianity did a particularly bad job of enforcing the human rights that can be intuited from the Bible. Biblically, human rights can be defended via the Bible. Animal rights are a different matter, however, since they are treated harshly throughout Scripture. On the other hand, atheists have every reason to think of future generations since this life is all there is.

Furthermore, atheists do not necessarily lose the value of life when it comes to sentient creatures because happiness is an attainable aspiration that we can all contribute to; We can all reduce the amount of suffering in the world if we choose to. The alternative is to contribute to suffering inadvertently. Some will not think that the arguments presented above are persuasive. In those cases, it will be enough to continue to urge slow thinking and shed light on the barbaric practices of factory-farming, its contributions to man-made climate change, and the striking similarities between other non-human animals and us.

Chapter 9

Christianity & Nuclear War

The heart is deceitful above all things, and desperately sick; who can understand it? Jer. 17:9

It is challenging to predict any behavior reliably today. Very few predicted Trump's inauguration or Brexit, for example. Many even doubted the uprising of Hitler, which was one reason he became so powerful in Europe. Few predicted the Russian annexation of Crimea; 9/11; the collapse of the Soviet Union; China's economic awakening; and other significant events in recent memory. We simply do not know what can happen and we are very bad at preventing calamities from occurring.

On July 16th, 2020, we remembered the 75th anniversary of the Trinity Nuclear Test, which took place in New Mexico in 1945. Only doomsday prophets could have predicted the rise of anything remotely similar to nuclear weapons at the time. Yet, here we are, 80 years later, still in awe of the capacity we have to destroy ourselves.

I touched on some of the historical problems that Christianity had in my previous chapter concerning wars from the Crusades, the Nine Years' War, the Thirty Years' War, the Eighty Years' War, the French Wars of Religion, the Wars of the Three Kingdoms, and the English Civil War. Christendom seriously failed to do a good job at avoiding wars.

Colonialism may well have also been a product of Christian teaching, although certainly based more on self-interest and a selfish reinterpretation of biblical texts. Some even argue that the World Wars may have had Christian origins. For example, Bertrand Russell claimed that The First World War was "wholly Christian in origin."[1] In it, French Christians, German Christians, and British Christians all thought against one another, believing that God favored their interests. Many wars seemed to be "wholly Christian," in Russell's words, in that they originated among Christians and were defended based on Christian dogma. Were these misinterpretations? And, more importantly, How would Christianity fare with the use of nuclear weapons today due to these "misinterpretations"?

A Just War?

Interestingly, the American exceptionalist ideology portrays American values as Christian values. But a careful look at history suggests a more complicated view. Christian apologists readily claim, for example, that the 20th-century is testimony to how secular values, or the "death of God," contributed to the Nazi Holocaust and other genocides of the century. They say that Nazi Germany, Fascist Italy, Soviet Russia, and the militaristic expansionism exhibited by Japan are all evidence of the futility of atheism. When, in fact, all of these regimes had very little to do with atheism.

Nazi Germany resembles a distinctly brainwashed utopian theism, if not outrightly, then certainly indirectly. Similarly, Stalin was worshipped as a god across the Soviet Union, and meanwhile, in Japan, regular citizens were not allowed to hear the Japanese Emperor's voice because of his god-like role as head of state.

The more troubling aspect is that America was far without faults during World War II, the Korean War, Vietnam War, and other proxy wars fought during the Cold War. It seems that the claim that war is an inevitable by-product of the lack of moral values is instead a testimony to a lack of historical understanding. For example, the oft-celebrated bombing of Hiroshima and Nagasaki, celebrated for ending the War, was far from necessary by all accounts. Some say that Japan would have fought long and hard in gorilla warfare, even to death. But in reality, due to the strong Soviet military pressure and the Japanese soldier's death-count in the Northern regions of Japan's fronts, Japan was likely to surrender since Hitler was already defeated and dead.

Indeed, we have some good reason to think that the nuclear bombing of Hiroshima and Nagasaki was a mixture of racism, eugenic superiority, military expansionism, and an inadvertent threat to Stalin of the military "might" of the United States. The bombing of Hiroshima and Nagasaki cost Japan approximately 200,000 lives, half of which died instantly, and half of which died from radiation burns and other injuries.[2] We also have some reason to believe that President Harry S. Truman did not even know that Hiroshima was a civilian city until weeks before. Few could have predicted such force from two bombs. Yet here we are, reckoning with such unimaginable power.

Along with others, Christians claim that war can be just and necessary, an argument originally promoted by Augustine in early Christendom. And there is some truth to the utility of war that most of us accept. We have good reason, for example, to think that Neville Chamberlain's pacifism during the 1930s, when Hitler invaded the demilitarized Rhineland and later Czechoslovakia and Poland, turned out to be ethically catastrophic.

Similarly, Benito Mussolini's attacks on Ethiopia and Japan's attacks and subjugation of mainland China should have been scrutinized heavily by the League of Nations. Today, similar fear of escalation leads many to ignore the human rights atrocities committed across the Globe, as is the case with the Uyghur Muslims, the Muslim Turkic minority in China in the Xinjiang region, the Kurds in Syria, or with Ukrainians and the annexation of Crimea by Russia in 2014 and subsequent war in the Donbas region in Ukraine.

The Cost of Lives of a Nuclear War

We cannot know for sure how detrimental a world-wide nuclear war would be, but estimates should concern us. Some of what are considered to be the most accurate estimates by experts show that a nuclear war poses three causes of destruction: blast, fire, and radiation.[3] We know that a nuclear explosion's blast manufactures a change in air pressure that crushes buildings near the blast, including most buildings within 3 km (1.9 miles) of a one-megaton hydrogen bomb.[4] The explosion would also produce "super-hurricane winds" that are strong enough to "destroy" people, trees, and utility poles.[5] Even houses as far out as 7.5 km (4.7 miles) would be damaged from such an explosion, if not entirely destroyed.[6] The Stanford University historian, Lynn Eddy, calculated that if a 300-kiloton nuclear weapon was dropped on the U.S. Department of Defense that "within tens of minutes, the entire area, approximately 40 to 65 square miles – everything within 3.5 or 6.4 miles of the Pentagon – would be engulfed in a mass fire," extinguishing all life and destroying what is left.[7] An explosion in a more densely populated region would cause much more damage to human life. Experts stress that India and Pakistan's long conflict is the largest threat to the outbreak of nuclear war since World War II.[8] Both India and Pakistan presently hold between 50 to 100 nuclear weapons. In that region, an outbreak of a nuclear war would see a densely populated area of the world devastated.[9]

However, these countries are not the only ones that possess nuclear weapons. The United Kingdom, France, Israel, China, North Korea, also possess nuclear weapons. Each country assures the rest of the world that these weapons are "secure, safe, and essential to security," however, each country is also suspicious of one another.[10] Many of these countries own nuclear weapons because of the international reputation and political influence that holding mass weapons of destruction garners.

For the Christian, all of these attacks are devastating because they destroy human life, and human life is sacred because we are made in God's image (Gen. 1:27). However, Christians also have a justification for a 'just war' within the Christian framework. And that is predominantly based on God's commandments and divine revelation. The secular person also justifies war but certainly not based on divine command.

The Just War

God ordains war throughout the Old Testament (Deut. 20:1, etc.). It should not come as a surprise then that Augustine and other early Church fathers thought it necessary to find a justification for war; If it's in the Bible, and God inspired our morality, then war must be just on certain occasions. In Psalms, it is written that:

> He trains my hands for war, so that my arms can bend a bow of bronze. Ps. 18:34

> Blessed be the Lord, my work, who trains my hands for war, and my fingers for battle. Ps. 144:1

Moses even proclaimed that if the Israelites would not fight against the Canaanites, it would be considered "sin":

> But Moses said to the people of Gad and to the people of Reuben, "Shall your brothers go to the war while you sit here? Why will you discourage the heart of the people of Israel from going over into the land that the LORD has given them? . . . If you will do this, if you will take up arms to go before the LORD for the war, and every armed man of you will pass over the Jordan before the LORD, until he has driven out his enemies from before him . . . then after that you shall return and be free of obligation to the LORD and to Israel, and this land shall be your possession before the LORD. But if you will not do so, behold, you have sinned

against the LORD, and be sure your sin will find you out." Num. 32:6-7, 20-23

The New Testament can also testify to the justness of war. Paul writes that rulers "bear the sword" to punish wrongdoers (Rom. 13:4), and Peter writes that the government is responsible for punishing "those who do evil" and praising "those who do good" (1 Pet. 2:14).

Although, these verses can testify to the spirit of the time, marked by conflict and dominion; They do not necessarily have to be commandments for today. But it is not as simple as that since even Jesus quotes the Old Testament to justify actions throughout the Gospels. So, we can expect that similar passages that justify war in the Old Testament warrant some attention from Christians making policy today.

To remind you, when Jesus said to "love your neighbor" (Matt. 22:39), he was quoting Leviticus 19:18 in the Old Testament. Therefore, we cannot merely dismiss these texts as outdated and non-applicable. John Calvin, whom we have mentioned throughout this book, recognized this and argued that:

> But kings and people must sometimes take up arms. . . . Indeed, if they rightly punish those robbers whose harmful acts have affected only a few, will they allow a whole country to be afflicted and devastated by robberies with impunity? For it makes no difference whether it be a king or the lowest of the common folk who invades a foreign country in which he has no right. . . . . All such must, equally, be considered as robbers and punished accordingly. Therefore . . . princes must be armed . . . to defend by war the dominions entrusted to their safekeeping, if at any time they are under enemy attack.[11]

Apart from the notion that war can be justified if ordained by God, which has not happened for some time now since that canon of the Bible has ended, the other argument for a just war for the Christian is self-defense. There are numerous cases in the Old Testament (Judg. 2:16-18; 1 Samuel 17; 2 Sam. 5:17-25, etc.). But God also uses war as a punishment toward the Israelites (e.g., Judg. 2:13-15).

So, war in the Bible is justified when (1) it is orchestrated by God, (2) in self-defense, and (3) as punishment.

Further Justifications for War

Over the centuries, many have agreed over the factors for a just war. They include:

1. *Just cause (Is the reason for war a morally defensible reason, such as in the case of a defense of a nation?)*
2. *Competent authority (Has the war been recognized by a competent authority within a nation?)*
3. *Comparative Justice (Can we tell for sure that the enemy's actions are morally wrong to the extent that going to war would be morally right?)*
4. *Right intention (Is the purpose of going to war to defend or to destroy?)*
5. *Last resort (Have other means of de-escalation and resolving the conflict been attempted?)*
6. *Probability of success (Can we know that the war will be won if instigated?)*
7. *Proportionality of projected results (Will the benefits of going to war outweigh the harms instilled as a result of going to war?)*
8. *Right spirit (Is the war partaken in with sorrow and hesitation?)*[12]

And, for the most part, as Grudem points out in *Christian Ethics*, biblical passages defend these ethical conditions for a just war. The question regarding nuclear war and the Christian is not entirely whether they find nuclear bombing just. For example, Grudem explains that the bombing of Hiroshima and Nagasaki ended the war and that estimates speculate that at least 500,000 American lives and hundreds of thousands of Japanese lives may have been saved.[13] He thus makes a utilitarian argument for the efficacy of nuclear weapons.

However, as I mentioned above, it is not entirely clear that the bombing was necessary to end the war. We know that Soviet attention was turned toward the Japanese imperialist force and that the Soviets had a much larger military strength than America since it almost single-handedly won the war against the Nazis in brutal combats fought on the Eastern Front, including the Battle of Kursk, the Battle of Moscow, the Second Battle of Kharkiv, and the deadliest of all, the Battle of Stalingrad, where more than 2 million soldiers and citizens are estimated to have lost their lives from both starvation and war.

To resolve how Christians will treat nuclear weapons, one could expect similar utilitarian arguments like the one given by Grudem above. They may also propose "just war" arguments in self-defense or to preserve values. Who knows? We have established that it is difficult to reliably predict behavior and evaluations, especially in politics and policy.

The Christian, along with the rest of the world, has just cause for war. It is hard to deny that stopping Hitler, Goebbels, Himmler, and others, at all costs was justifiable because of their vitriolic hatred of ethnic minorities and the supremacist ideologies that would have covered most of the world, indoctrinating and suppressing millions. The Christian, if upholding the secular consensus, will be able to prevent any unnecessary conflicts from arising. However, that capability is not at all the direct result of Christian doctrine but rather in the personal responsibility of individuals and the collective to maintain what is best for the highest number of people.

Chapter 10

Atheism & Nuclear War

It should be obvious to anyone reading this book that atheism does not have anything specific to say about nuclear war. Atheism naturally cannot say anything about an issue that does not relate to the existence or non-existence of gods. However, an atheist position very well may take a position for the complete eradication of the Christian concept for 'just war' based on divine command as was explored in the previous chapter. For the atheist, any justification for war on the basis of God's commandment, as was common throughout the Old Testament, is contemptible.

We know from cinema and books that nuclear war of cataclysmic proportions is very much a threat. The Cold War saw an influx of cinema related to the dangers of nuclear war. *On the Beach* (1959) creates a fictitious scenario where Australians are forced to face the fact that all life will end in a few months; *Threads* (1984) depicts a world where in Sheffield, England, working-class citizens are battling the long-term effects of nuclear war; *The Day After* (1983) shows the aftermath of a nuclear holocaust on the life of residents in a small-town in eastern Kansas; *By Dawn's Early Light* (1990) features a scenario where Turkey fires a nuclear missile at the USSR; and so forth. Films filled the imaginations of everyday viewers of what might come to be if the USSR and the USA, the two major superpowers in the middle of an arms-race, collide.

But how real are these threats? In the previous chapter, we looked at some of the horrors that would follow if a nuclear war took place. I want to explore that threat further and point out why a utilitarian argument for nuclear weapons is almost as equally preposterous as one from divine command.

How Real is the Threat of Nuclear War?

Officially, only a few countries possess nuclear weapons in the first place. And the number of nuclear weapons has been drastically reduced from 65,000 in 1986 to about 26,000 in 2007, 96% of which are owned by the United States and Russia.[1] As of January 2007, the U.S. owns 10,000 nuclear weapons and Russia up to 15,000.[2] It should be pointed out that the number of these weapons are still concerning. Indeed, even if only 100 of these nuclear weapons exploded, they would have the potential to cover the Earth in lethal smoke, "ushering in a years-long nuclear winter, with global droughts and massive crop failures."[3] In 2007, Russia even tested a submarine-based missile that carries six nuclear warheads and is able to travel over 6000 miles, being able to reach the United States.[4] But it is unlikely that Russia would use any of these weapons. Nikita Khrushchev, after taking over from Stalin and learning about the dangers of nuclear weapons in 1953 said, "I couldn't sleep for several days. Then I became convinced that we could never possibly use these weapons, and when I realized that I was able to sleep again."[5]

Despite world leaders recognizing that we can never use these weapons, these bombs are tested readily. Since 1945, "at least eight countries have conducted more than 2,000 nuclear test explosions" including 1,030 by the US.[6] About one-fourth of these "killed" or "sickened" military personnel conducting the tests and citizens who were in close proximity to the tests. The 1996 Comprehensive Test Ban Treaty was then established to prevent further nuclear tests due to the harm done to citizens. The treaty was signed by the U.S. and 183 other states and ratified by 168 (last reviewed July 2020).[7] Alarmingly, it has as of July 2020 not been ratified by 8 key nations, including China, India, Pakistan, North Korea, Israel, Iran, Egypt, and the United States.

Blue Blair, the former Minuteman launch officer and currently the president of the World Security Institute claims that if Russia and the U.S. "sent the launch order right now, without any warning or preparation, thousands of nuclear weapons – the equivalent in explosive firepower of about 70,000 Hiroshima bombs – could be unleashed within a few minutes."[8]

Blair explains what this could look like in vivid detail:

If early warning satellites or ground radar detected missiles in flight, both sides would attempt to assess whether a real nuclear attack was under way within a strict and short deadline. Under Cold War procedures that are still in practice today, early warning crews manning their consoles 24/7 have only three minutes to reach a preliminary conclusion. Such occurrences happen on a daily basis, sometimes more than once per day. . . . . if an apparent nuclear missile threat is perceived, then an emergency teleconference would be convened between the president and his top nuclear advisers. On the US side, the top officer on duty at Strategic Command in Omaha, Neb., would brief the president on his nuclear options and their consequences. That officer is allowed all of 30 seconds to deliver this briefing.

Then the US or Russian president would have to decide whether to retaliate, and since the command systems on both sides have long been geared for launch-on-warning, the presidents would have little spare time if they desired to get retaliatory nuclear missiles off the ground before they – and possibly the presidents themselves – were vaporized. On the US side, the time allowed to decide would range between zero and 12 minutes, depending on the scenario. Russia operates under even tighter deadlines because of the short flight time of US Trident submarine missiles on forward patrol in the North Atlantic.[9]

In *The Russia Trap*, George Beebe encapsulates the literature on the potential of nuclear warfare between Russia and the United States. Beebe writes that the perceptions of existential threat are "raising the stakes in the US-Russian relationship well beyond the limited geopolitical competition that should flow from the objective mix of conflicting and compatible American and Russian interests" (29). Beebe, along with others, believes that both Russia and the U.S. have good reasons to think that each are trying to undermine one another's sovereignty.

If a nuclear war outbroke between the U.S. and Russia, an American attack on Russia would require approximately 1300 warheads. If used, they would within hours of the explosion cause lethal ramifications for an area larger than France the United Kingdom. Anywhere from 11 to 17 million civilians would lose their lives.[10] Government studies also purport that if Russia would respond to an attack of this sort with typical procedures, between 35 and 77% of the U.S. population (approximately 105-230 million citizens) and between 20 and 40% of the Russian population (approximately 28-56 million citizens) could be killed.[11] Joseph Cirincione writes in *Global Catastrophic Risks* that if this were to happen, "It would be doubtful that either the United States or Russia would ever recover as viable nation states."[12]

Kennedy himself said in 1962 that "there is not going to be any winner of the next war. No one who is a rational man can possibly desire to see hostilities break out, particularly between the major powers which are equipped with nuclear weapons."[13]

Hypothetical Disasters and Unwarranted Fears

These predictions are obviously worst-case scenarios. But people are still worried today especially with the increasing tendency to use nuclear energy as an antidote to fossil fuel. In the previous chapter, we looked at Grudem's utilitarian argument for the use of nuclear weapons in World War II. For Grudem and for others that propose this argument, dropping the bombs on Hiroshima and Nagasaki was necessary to prevent further death. As was mentioned before, there are prescient questions over whether Japan would surrender because of Stalin's invasion from the North. And this is precisely why utilitarian arguments for the use of nuclear weapons come across as inhumane and undiplomatic.

If anything, we could argue that the use of nuclear weapons should be made illegal in the first place. First and foremost, the risks of using them are far too high, as political and ideological opponents such as Russia and the United States both possess large arsenals of nuclear weapons. It is unlikely that countries would give up their nuclear arsenal, however. Many see the utility of having these weapons because sovereignty and autonomy is more likely to be maintained. The harsh reality is that we must continuously advocate for disarmament and not be discouraged by the inevitable slow progress when discussing these large issues.

But the real question is whether we are exaggerating the case for worrying about nuclear war in the 21st century. As Steven Pinker points out in *Enlightenment Now*, "Sowing fear about hypothetical disasters, far from safeguarding the future of humanity, can endanger it."[14] Once you know about the close calls we have had in the past with nuclear disaster, it is hard not to presuppose that few in positions of control over these weapons know what they are doing. The experts do worry about these issues.

Close Calls and Warranted Fears

So, should *we* worry about nuclear war? Or are these simply "hypothetical disasters" as Pinker proposes? We actually have very good reason to be up in arms about how little control over nuclear weapons there is. Let's have a look at some of the close-calls.

In 1979, on November 9th, at 3 a.m. screens at four U.S. command centers lit up with a full-scale Soviet nuclear attack. The U.S. only had a few minutes before responding to this attack before their own missiles were destroyed. As was mentioned above, often the response time to these attacks is as little as 12 minutes. President Reagan reported, "The Russians sometimes kept submarines off our East Coast with nuclear missiles that could turn the White House into a pile of radioactive rubble within six to eight minutes. *Six minutes* to decide how to respond to a blip on a radar scope and decide whether to release Armageddon! How can anyone apply reason at a time like that?"[15] In this particular case, after commanders prepared nuclear bombers for their attack and called on fighter planes to meet the Russian bombers, the early-warning systems turned out to be a false alarm. In fact, the screens were merely showing a simulation of a Soviet onslaught from an exercise that was mistakenly given to live computer systems. We were lucky. This serious accident is now known as the "Training Tape Incident."[16]

Few realize how serious these incidents really are. They think that nuclear war is a threat that movies depict to keep citizens entertained. In reality, these decisions are made in a matter of minutes with very few people in the room. Late at night on September 26th, 1983, a similar incident occurred from the Soviet side. Just past midnight, Stanislav Petrov, a duty officer, saw five ICBMs launching from the United States and by training was instructed to report these incidents to the authorities. He reportedly told the authorities that there were too few missiles, making it unlikely for the attack to be real. In the end, this false alarm was caused by sunlight glinting off clouds, which the Soviet satellite systems picked up as threats. Many say that Petrov was responsible for saving the world that night because he refused to launch missiles in response. If the system reported closer to a hundred missiles, Petrov may have called for a nuclear response, however.[17] We were seriously close to a real nuclear catastrophe.

Similar cases such as the ones mentioned above happened after the end of the Cold War, as was the case with the "Norwegian Rocket Incident" on January 25, 1995. In this case, then Russian President, Yeltsin, was called to make a decision to respond to an alert which then turned out to be another false alarm caused by a Norwegian scientific rocket that was launched to study the northern lights.[18] Indeed, according to a U.S. Department of Defense report, there have been 32 known cases of nuclear weapons accidents.[19] These range from nuclear weapons accidentally falling from a B-36 bomber over New Mexico in 1957 to bomber planes crashing mid-air in 1958 near Savannah, Georgia, or a fighter jet carrying a 1-megaton bomb and falling off a US-aircraft carrier close to Japan in 1965 which has since never been recovered.[20]

Most alarmingly, the U.S. has policies in effect that give full control to the American President over nuclear weapons. With unstable presidents like Richard Nixon, who struggled with alcohol abuse, and Kennedy, who had medication problems, and more recently with Donald Trump, who implied that he would use nuclear weapons against North Korea with "fire and fury like the world has never seen," we have good reason to worry.[21] As William J. Perry writes in *The Button: The New Nuclear Arms Race and Presidential Power from Truman to Trump*, "[U]nder current policy, there is no realistic way to stop a determined president from going nuclear."[22]

The only solution it seems is wide disarmament and policies that will prevent nuclear weapons from existing in the first place. The 21st century is one where we will have to meet these threats and seek deescalation at all costs.

Part C

Our Everything

Chapter 11

The Christian & the Meaning of Life

One of the first questions that dawned on me as I abandoned my faith in early adulthood, was that I was now "free." Along with this feeling, I remember that this "freedom" had an unnatural sting to it. For some reason, I could not find it fulfilling. Looking back I now realize that it wasn't simply that abandoning my ideology led to my unfulfillment but rather, it was that I did not have a community that I belonged to. Earlier in life, my faith granted me a community. That is why whenever I tell young Christians if they want to see whether their "faith" is real, I urge them to abandon their Christian communities; They will quickly realize how much of their faith depends on those closest to them. Similarly, I readily admit that if I ever lose my closest friends that are nonbelievers and join Christian communities, it may become the case that I return to my previous faith. I briefly explained how little our reasoning impacts our opinions and I stand by those views. Although, I would like to believe that I would keep my agnosticism; It is difficult to see myself coming back to the faith of my youth.

The seeming meaninglessness of life is not off-limits by Christian theology. Indeed, some may argue that one of the central themes to the Bible is how it provides Christians a place to belong in relation to God and thus gives meaning to individuals within the context of eternity. This may be true.

Throughout life, we struggle from successes to failures, job to unemployment, relationship to betrayal. We are never content and we let the world know, either by silently accepting our fate and becoming consumers that swallow each bit of media content whole, or by purchasing endless amounts of clothes to satisfy our thirst for novelty, or by indulging in pleasure that rarely satisfies. This is all because suffering is the consistent presence in every single person's life. Everyone you know will one day pass away. Your body will start to deteriorate. Your mind will lose its ability to focus and remember things clearly. Happy moments seem fleeting and the responsibilities of life are overbearing. What are we to do in the midst of this?

The world certainly has some problem with what seems to be an endless pursuit for pleasure. And the Bible is not without its fair share of answers to our predicament. In fact, this question is beautifully explored by Solomon in *Ecclesiastes* in a strikingly honest passage. One of Solomon's conclusions from this passage will be familiar to most who have read the Bible, "all is vanity and a chasing after wind" (Ecclesiastes 1:14). Solomon continues:

> I said in my heart, "Come now, I will test you with pleasure; enjoy yourself." But behold, this also was vanity. I said of laughter, "It is mad," and of pleasure, "What use is it?" I searched with my heart how to cheer my body with wine—my heart still guiding me with wisdom—and how to lay hold on folly, till I might see what was good for the children of man to do under heaven during the few days of their life. I made great works. I built houses and planted vineyards for myself. I made myself gardens and parks, and planted in them all kinds of fruit trees. I made myself

pools from which to water the forest of growing trees. I bought male and female slaves, and had slaves who were born in my house. I had also great possessions of herds and flocks, more than any who had been before me in Jerusalem. I also gathered for myself silver and gold and the treasure of kings and provinces. I got singers, both men and women, and many concubines, the delight of the sons of man.

So I became great and surpassed all who were before me in Jerusalem. Also my wisdom remained with me. And whatever my eyes desired I did not keep from them. I kept my heart from no pleasure, for my heart found pleasure in all my toil, and this was my reward for all my toil. Then I considered all that my hands had done and the toil I had expended in doing it, and behold, all was vanity and a striving after wind, and there was nothing to be gained under the sun. Ecclesiastes 2:1-11

For the Christian, fulfillment is only found in God. We are to dwell on His word, day and night, as the psalmist tells us and forget about our troubles because our trust and delight is in God (Psalm 1:2). The opening line to the best-selling hardback book in the United States, *Purpose Driven Life*, by Rick Warren, is that this life is not about you. Warren suggests that one of the main problems with society today in the West is that we have made it about self-actualization at all costs.

In the West, life is unfulfilling if you are not the center of it, the protagonist in your story. We are told this by movies and books alike. From when we are small children, we are told we are "special" and that we will do great things. Once we enter our early adult years, however, we slowly begin to realize that few things about us seem special and that most people feel the same way about their "unique" capabilities.

In many ways, the Christian view that life is principally about finding God and delighting in Him can be freeing. Secular thinkers would do well to look at why Warren's insights into living are so well-received by the Christian community. It may be the case that self-absorption is harmful. And the West, with its self-centered celebrity-obsession, may feel better if it embraces it. The question then is whether humanism can lead to less self-indulgence and whether Christianity has a unique way out from the perils of materialism.

The Problems With Individualism

As much as the Christian can focus on these earthly things, they are citizens of heaven and rightly should also prioritize eternal things. The desire to spread the Gospel because of the terrifying realities of hell are apparent. Jesus does not leave room for lukewarm Christianity. As is written in Revelations: "[B]ecause you are lukewarm—neither hot nor cold—I am about to spit you out of my mouth" (3:14–16). In another passage Jesus says, "In the same way, on the outside you appear to people as righteous but on the inside you are full of hypocrisy and wickedness" (Matthew 23:25–28).

In *The Good Life*, Colson explains that the logic of individualism is "suicidal" and "paradoxical." For Colson and other Christians, "If we belong only to ourselves, then nonexistence is the only solution when we find life too great a burden."[1] And there is some truth to this statement. However, Colson presupposes that atheists are automatically perilously individualistic. As we saw from previous chapters, individualism brought a lot of good with it. Today, society is becoming individualistic in a different way. As we saw, our face-to-face interactions are deteriorating. Furthermore, society promises the "American Dream" to those that ambitiously pursue a life of work and fulfilment through career success. But many have now understood the vacuous nature of these promises.

One of the biggest problems with individualism, according to the Christian perspective, is not only that life is unfulfilling but that because life is temporary and that everyone will inevitably die, life cannot be meaningful in and of itself.

Thus, Timothy Keller writes, "Death strips us of everything that makes life meaningful."[2] For the Christian, death is the enemy and Jesus has slain it (1 Corinthians 15:26). Furthemore, Christians have the promise of an afterlife and let's be honest, an afterlife certainly sounds nice. But along with that it is also a contemptible doctrine since so many will suffer for eternity. But we will get to that. As Keller points out, "While secularism offers no hope for any life after death, most religions do."[3]

The Christian Community

I looked at some of the ways that Christians can excel at providing a sense of community to others. That is why, as Robert Wright estimates, Paul's evangelism was so successful because he made sure to include every sin imageable under restricted behavior in order to prevent strife from within the community.

As we saw in our chapter on Christian moral insight, there is something to be said about how Christianity can emphasize communal living. Charles Colson recognizes this and writes, "To live the good, we have to understand how much our lives belong to others and what a good thing that is."[4] Although with this emphasis on community, we also know how exclusive the Christian teaching for community really is. This is for one, because the neighbor does not apply as broadly as we previously thought, as I touched on before. But also, because of the exclusive morality that disregards minorities. Colson himself in the same book proves my point. When he touches on "homosexual couples" he writes, "In many ways, those who suffer from same-sex attraction find their sexuality leads to an obsession with self. For example, homosexual couples often celebrate how they look, emphasizing everything visual, from fashion to haircuts to body sculpting. ... As homosexuals grow older, many become desperate to regain their youth symbolically through affairs with young men. Others find they cannot cope with their own idealized self-images. The sexual goround wears itself out, and they suffer from depression, loneliness, and despair."[5] Although, this may say something about the disturbing way self-absorption can harm our mental health, it says little about why same-sex attraction is wrong. The author was not aware of this and it shows.

Making Sense of Suffering

One of the reasons why we are so preoccupied with the meaning of life is because we experience suffering and want to make sense of it. Biblically, suffering can be explained a number of ways.

At least originally, suffering was the curse issued by God on Adam and Eve for eating the fruit of knowledge in the Garden of Eden. Eve and all women that followed her, were punished with painful childbirth, which may be one of the most painful experiences any human could feel. Adam and all men following him, were meanwhile subjected to working the dreaded soil, subject to the seasons, famine, pests, and dangerous predators.

For the prophets in the Old Testament, suffering was also the direct result of God's people disobeying God. One of the reasons why upon the Jewish people's exodus from Egypt, God's people wandered on the desert was because they were disobedient to God. Moses says that God will punish the Israelites if they disobey God (Deut. 28:16-28). Later God inflicted suffering on them as is recalled by Isaiah, Jeremiah, Amos, and the other prophets.

The Christian certainly prides themselves in making sense of suffering, claiming that God has a reason for everything, ultimately meant for the good of His people (Romans 8:28). The Christian waits for the afterlife which puts these "trivial" moments of suffering into perspective. For Paul, Job, and Jesus alike suffering is meant to showcase the glory of God. Our suffering is the same.

What the Christian has a difficult time figuring out is why suffering is directly used by God both as punishment and as a means to edify His people. The New Testament view is largely the same as the one found in the Old Testament. Jesus had to come as the ultimate atonement for suffering.

Evangelism

The life of the Christian is not only meaningful in theory, in that you have a way to face suffering and expect eternal rewards for your suffering on earth; It is also meaningful in practice, namely in that it gives people a coherent message to follow: evangelism.

If you take Jesus' claims seriously, your life *needs* to replicate his life in terms of sacrifice. As a Christian, you need to take his claims seriously. Every moment of your day should be inspired by the Word of God. Jesus requires you to suffer for the Gospel in order to be His follower. Jesus tells you to "hate your mother" in comparison to the love you have for God and forsake earthly pleasures (Luke 14:26).

Jesus said to make disciples of all nations, baptizing them in the name of the Father, Son, and Holy Spirit. This call was also not unique to the disciples. Paul repeatedly calls for the spreading of the Gospel. As much as a children's life in Africa is important, it is arguably more important to provide the good news of Christ to African children so they won't "burn" forever, than to simply provide a proper education to them.

Why would Christians throw away their lives like this? It's because their life is not their own. It was bought with a price and that was Christ's blood (Gal 3:13). If God is all-powerful and sovereign, how should we reject His will. How do we really say "no" to God, or ask him *why have you made me this way?* (Rom 9:20)

Focusing on Sin and Hell

Bertrand Russell once said that religion is based "primarily and mainly upon fear." Russell was a staunch opponent of most Christian teaching as we have seen throughout the book. And there is some truth to this statement. The biblical scholar, Bart D. Ehrman quotes one of the earliest examples of apocalyptic writing found in the *Apocalypse of Peter*, where Jesus gives Peter a glimpse into what life is like for unbelievers in eternity.

In the realms of the damned Peter sees blasphemers

hanged by their tongues over eternal flames. Men who committed adultery are similarly suspended, but by their genitals. Women who have performed abortions on themselves are sunk in excrement up to their necks forever. Those who slandered Christ and doubted his righteousness have their eyes perennially burned out with red-hot irons. Those who worship idols are chased by demons off high canyons, time and again. Slaves who disobeyed their masters are forced to gnaw their tongues incessantly while being burned by fire.[6]

Christians will say that the account of hell in the Bible is not as horrific as this account. Remember, it seems that a good reason to take evangelism seriously is not only because God called on the disciples to do so but most importantly because of the picture of hell seen in the Bible. In the Christian hell, "the wicked" are thrown into a "blazing furnace, where there will be weeping and gnashing of teeth" (Matthew 13:50). This furnace has a "fire [that] never goes out" (Mark 9:43). The Bible features a number of terrifying passages that in some way confirm Russell's presumption that, at least to some extent, Christianity has historically relied on fear. Ehrman writes that "There is a good deal of evidence to suggest that, far more than the glories of heaven, it was the tortures of hell that convinced potential converts."[7] And the Bible testifies to this reality:

> But the cowardly, the unbelieving, the vile, the murderers, the sexually immoral, those who practice magic arts, the idolaters and all liars—they will be consigned to the fiery lake of burning sulfur. This is the second death. Revelation 21:8

> Then they will go away to eternal punishment, but the righteous to eternal life. Matthew 25:46

> They will be punished with everlasting destruction

and shut out from the presence of the Lord and from the glory of his might. 2 Thessalonians 1:9

If your hand causes you to stumble, cut it off. It is better for you to enter life maimed than with two hands to go into hell, where the fire never goes out. Mark 9:43

Then they will go away to eternal punishment, but the righteous to eternal life. Matthew 25:46

The wicked go down to the realm of the dead, all the nations that forget God. Psalm 9:17

They will be punished with everlasting destruction and shut out from the presence of the Lord and from the glory of his might. 2 Thessalonians 1:9

[A]nd throw them into the blazing furnace, where there will be weeping and gnashing of teeth. Matthew 13:50

In a similar way, Sodom and Gomorrah and the surrounding towns gave themselves up to sexual immorality and perversion. They serve as an example of those who suffer the punishment of eternal fire. Jude 1:17

Then he will say to those on his left, 'Depart from me, you who are cursed, into the eternal fire prepared for the devil and his angels. Matthew 25:4

For if God did not spare angels when they sinned, but sent them to hell, putting them in chains of darkness to be held for judgment. 2. Peter 2:4

The Roman historian, Ramsay MacMullen, has called Christian accounts of the afterlife "the only sadistic literature I am aware of in the ancient world."[8] It was Augustine himself who said that it cannot be that "someone comes to us with the wish to become a Christian who has not been struck by some fear of God."[9] The risks to this teaching are obvious. Some studies even suggest that parents that threat children with God's punishment can put them at risk to develop excessive self-blaming, for example.[10] So it would make sense that if Christians excessively focus on these passages of hell and in their personal lives that they could exhibit some unhealthy behavior.

Along with the Christian obsession with hell in the medieval world, Christians were also fearful of the Devil. William Nichols argues that the Devil may have even been more real to the medieval mind than God himself.[11] We can't know for certain. But we know that the Devil's sole purpose was to bring down the Christian; and the more holy the Christian, the more likely that he would come visit them.[12]

If Christianity gave meaning to the individual in the medieval era, it was because their focus was to avoid eternal damnation and push away the "cunning smell," "sulphurous smell," and "horns, tail, and all."[13] As with human rights and the tumultuousness of Christian values, Christianity's understanding of the meaning of life changes throughout the centuries. From the way I see it, the existence of hell and the mission to keep people out in order to know the creator of the universe is the central component to the life of a Christian. Indeed, if one believes in hell, it would be difficult to focus on anything else.

The Christian Message

The central component to evangelism is the understanding of hell and the gravity of not spreading the Gospel. This is explored most infamously perhaps by Jonathan Edwards in his sermon, "Sinners in the Hands of an Angry God." For Edwards, we are but a spider on a last strip of web hovering over eternal abyss; Anything can happen, and we will fall into hell for eternity. Thus, he calls for urgency, understandably so.

This all may seem fairly appalling and cruel. But it is biblical. In the Christian world sin is cosmic treason, intentional willful defiance of the Creator, it is to create war on God. It is not just that we disobey God, it is that we are in a state of constant disobedience. We worship anything and everything, but the true God.

Apart from this, there is also a beauty in the Christian message that lures people in. There is a beginning (Genesis—the fall), there is a middle (Jesus—the redemption), and an end (Jesus' second coming—the coming of the Kingdom of Heaven). This compelling narrative along with the social communities that form around such narratives surely provides some meaning to the lives of Christians. However, that does not say anything about the validity of the Christian message, for obvious reasons.

The doctrine of hell and the message of the Gospel bring both bad and good to the lives of Christians. Historically, hell may have been the driving force for conversion along with the ubiquitous terrifying presence of demons in the world. Today, we are not so petrified unless we've just watched *The Exorcist* or any other movie disturbingly portraying the "wrath" of demons. As secular thinkers, we should not merely look at Christian promises of the afterlife with contempt. Rather, we should understand them. The world in the end is a lonely place with too much suffering. The next question I want to explore, is whether atheists have a way of facing the suffering of this world.

Chapter 12
The Atheist & the Meaning of LIfe

Western society has flourished in many ways since the 1960s. With this social flourishing, growing individualism, and weakening face-to-face interactions, we also see a steady increase in depression, anxiety, meaninglessness, and all the rest. Society is burdened with an aggressive emptiness. This burden is by no means new, but we are seeing it accelerate in recent years. That can explain the popularity of self-help books. However, civilization has seen discussions like this since the writings of the Stoics, Epicureans, and Confucians. There is a lot of wisdom in these ancient texts that, for the most part, preceded Christian teaching. However, as I pointed out in my previous chapter, there is also a lot of wisdom in Christian teaching, and we should not dismiss it entirely.

Secularism indeed does have a problem. The problem from the way I see it, is that we have not prescribed reasons to have social lives as Christians have. For the Christian, the community is everything; The Church is Christ's bride and has a vital role in God's redemptive plan. For the atheist, our contributions are less spiritual; We simply exist in one another's space and learn to cohabitate with the least number of squabbles possible for our well-being.

Albert Camus, in his book *The Myth of Sisyphus*, calls the dilemma for the atheist of facing eternal nothingness as "the absurd." For Camus, Sisyphus' condemnation from the gods was in that "They had thought with some reason that there is no more dreadful punishment than futile and hopeless labor."[1] In a way, we are all then condemned to a similar life where we are sent to hopeless labor to obtain pleasure that never satisfies. Let's explore that topic and see whether these metaphors for life are expansive enough for the precarious human condition.

Can an Atheist Have a Meaning of Life?

The meaning of life for the atheist is simple: it can be anything. This, however, can both be a blessing and a curse. Many automatically think that this is a burden. In some way, they are implying in the same way that the aristocrats did to the peasantry class in the 18th century, that freedom is, above all, a curse and only Christ can free us from the curse of our precarious or "absurd" lives.

Humanism shifted the focus of attention from the monarch, God, and the elite, to the individual. Consequently, people had access to God, not through the Church, tradition, or the Pope, but rather by reading, analyzing, and interpreting texts personally – as individuals. It can be argued that humanism and Protestantism coincided in this era of rediscovery.

Existentialist thinkers such as Jean-Paul Sartre argued that the individual, not the establishment, has the sole power to define themselves. Sartre, therefore, dismisses *a priori* claims about human nature and argues for constructivism. In constructivist thought, human beings design their reality. Existentialists claim that the subjective is more important than the objective, or the establishment, in defining individual reality. Humanist existentialism argued that the concept of subjectivity provided freedom to citizens.

As I argued in the previous chapter, the Christian ideology is somewhat crippled by (1) the reality of hell, and (2) the mission to spread the Gospel. On the other hand, the humanist can easily be crippled by the ultimate freedom that they have. In one way, yes, you can do any drug you want or steal whatever you want, or hurt whomever you please, and face no apparent benevolent objection. However, your freedom to do any drug of your choice can also cripple your life, making the comforts of a healthy family and friends unlikely. So, the atheist is not entirely without punishment if they chose to participate in "sinful" or harmful behavior. The problem with individualism, then, is that as an ideology, it can foster leaving homes, communities, and cities in exchange for fulfillment in careers that are isolating and ultimately detrimental to one's mental health.[2]

I have already discussed whether atheists can be moral in my chapter on morality and atheism. The logical next step is whether the atheist is morally compelled in the same way as the Christian is, to a life of meaning. There are many ways to analyze this question.

As I have argued before, we are storytelling animals; the stories we tell each other determine our reality, how we perceive our differences, how we treat our neighbors, and whether we bomb each other and cause vast amounts of needless suffering. It is as the anthropologist Clifford Geertz wrote, "man is an animal suspended in webs of significance that he himself has spun."[3] We can tell ourselves any number of stories that make our lives significant, and we can furthermore tell ourselves that our lives are unique because of the story we've told ourselves. However, with the number of compelling stories, it is unlikely that our story can ever be universalized. You may find the Gospel's mission both stimulating and fulfilling, but that does not necessarily suggest that anyone should partake in that mission as well.

That is not to say that everything is futile and meaningless but rather that we can decide what is of significance, as Sartre and Camus would have us do. In the words of Camus, we must imagine Sisyphus happy. It is up to him to decide whether he will perceive his precarious situation in a way that would prescribe meaning to it or think of it as meaningless.

Is Happiness Attainable at All?

Camus' analogy of Sisyphus is rather dark and gloomy. I do not think of it as the best analogy for life since life can also bring a lot of good if we set ourselves up for it in the best ways. Jonathan Haidt touches on many important ways to boost your likelihood of happiness in his book *The Happiness Hypothesis*. In it, he writes that each of us has a unique genetic predisposition for happiness, a "natural and usual state of tranquility."[4] Haidt explains that both lottery winners and paraplegics return to their baseline level of happiness within a year, which is predominantly predetermined by their genetics.[5] In the words of Haidt, "In the long run, it doesn't much matter what happens to you. Good fortune or bad, you will always return to your happiness setpoint – your brain's default level of happiness – which was determined largely by your genes."[6] It seems then that the pursuit of pleasure and money at all costs is futile and that happiness must come from elsewhere.

Social Animals

Some research indicates that religious people are happier than non-religious people on average, largely because of the religious community and social connections these communities provide.[7] The importance of social ties is well-documented in sociology. Along with our social lives come the obligations we have to one another, which are correlated with healthy behavior.

Emile Durkheim, one of the founders of sociology, observed in the late 19th century that people with fewer social obligations were more prone to suicide.[8] At the time, Durkheim compared the social commitments of Protestants, Catholics, and Jews and found that Protestants had the most freedom. They were also more likely to commit suicide, "Having strong social relationships strengthens the immune system, extends life (more than does quitting smoking), speeds recovery from surgery, and reduces the risks of depression and anxiety disorders."[9]

The sociologist Glen Elder, who studied the traumatic effect the Great Depression and World War II brought on citizens, similarly found that both children and adults with strong social groups responded better to these crises than those without them; "Social networks didn't just reduce suffering, they offered avenues for finding meaning and purpose."[10] Therefore, we can safely assume that we need, first and foremost, social groups as atheists, something that we have not stressed as much as our religious counterparts. Only then can we begin to find fulfillment in other areas of life.

Attention and the Present Moment

In Sam Harris' book, *Waking Up: A Guide to Spirituality Without Religion*, Harris asks whether happiness is attainable "before anything happens" in the middle of pain and suffering, disease and death.[11] He touches on a crucial element to our unfortunate human condition. I recall it most clearly from the summer of 2019. I was working every day, I had three days off in three months, and I worked long 50 to 60 weeks. I have had other periods like this in my life, but I recall this to be among my more unhappy ones.

During this turbulent time, I remember feeling lost and unhappy. I picked up Harris' book because I remember it being influential on my state of mind when I previously read it. This question struck me as the crux of the problem of the human condition. What was the reason I was working so much? I wanted to be happy later on, afford university, and live without financial worries through my semesters. I realized that I should not be unhappy in the moment because the moment, despite how tedious and seemingly insignificant, is *all* there is. Or, as Sam Harris put it, "attention is your true source of wealth" (paraphrased). He writes, "Your mind is the basis of everything you experience and of every contribution you make to the lives of others."[12]

There are many different ways to "train" the mind to think in this way, to experience life in the moment despite how miserable or fulfilling it is. We either cling to brief moments of euphoria for too long and forget that life cannot only be made of happy moments, or we are stifled by the death of a family member or close friend. If we do not have the luxury of stories that assure us that eternity awaits, we are faced with the challenge to find pleasure in the moment despite what the moment carries with it. Or, as Harris puts it, "[W]e are seeking fulfillment while at the mercy of changing experience."[13] In Harris' view, fulfillment is precisely found in realizing that each moment of suffering and happiness are both just appearances in consciousness. The thing is, these appearances and how seriously we take them, or our "habitual identification with thought," is in the words of Harris, "a primary source of suffering."[14] For Harris, meditation, the "training" of the mind, is one way to help remind ourselves in each moment, that this thought is only as real as we permit it to be.

Others have already preached this message long before Harris has. Stoics like Marcus Aurelius and Seneca recognized this some 2,000 years ago. Aurelius' *Meditations*, a post-mortem collection of journals, are filled with sober reflections on the human experience, guiding Aurelius to live in the present, not to expect much from others, and live life acknowledging that life will come to an end. Buddha and Epictetus both adopted similar principles almost entirely independent of one another. Buddha taught that earthly attachments would bring suffering into your life, Epictetus taught that we could never control outcomes, only our inner reactions. In other words, these ancient thinkers found that "Happiness comes from within, and it cannot be found by making the world conform to your desires."[15]

The End for the Atheist

What is the end then for the atheist? Is it Hitler's Nazi ideology? Or is it a peaceful utopia that is inclusive and accepting of each other's differences? As you may have guessed from this book's theme, the answer is not clear and can differ depending on how you answer the question. We can know what to do and not to do, however. We do not have to pursue ephemeral sensations, like pleasure, for the sake of pleasure solely. We can find fulfillment and meaning in a life where suffering prevails over other sensations with paying closer attention, with loving relationships with one another, and a careful reflection of life. These things are not easy, and that is why we need one another.

In the end, life is wondrous, and a mystery, and living in perpetual awe of life is enough for a cause of celebration and astonishment. In the words of Michael Shermer,

> We are, in fact, made *from* the stars. Our atoms were forged in the interior of ancient stars that ended their lives in spectacular paroxysms of supernova explosions that dispersed those atoms into space, where they coalesced into new solar systems with planets, life, and sentient beings capable of such sublime knowledge and moral wisdom.[16]

Afterword

Who Won?

This was not meant to be a competition. Clearly, many will be reading this book in that way. Instead, I meant for us to understand each other's differences and learn how to engage with the opposing side from a position of understanding rather than contempt.

My goal was to edify rather than tear down. When I engage with someone in conversation, I will never want it to be to harm and malign them. This malicious approach may sell and it may garner followers as we can see from the popularity of opportunists across social media. But if we revoke to these popularity tactics, how can we call ourselves integral, honest, and caring to our fellow beings? We need to unite in the 21st century and the only way to do so is to change our vocabulary, seek to understand those we fundamentally disagree with, and above all, be kind.

I hope you were able to learn something new from this book and I am thankful for you taking the time to read it.

My Thanks

My largest thanks, from the bottom of my heart, is to my close friend, Anastasiia Lapatina. She has been there for me and encouraged me like no one else, from carefully reading the first drafts and providing detailed comments to dealing with my imposter syndrome and childish insecurities. I am so lucky to have met someone as wonderfully ambitious, talented, and warm-hearted as my friend, Ana. Your laugh, energy, and heart helps me believe in people. I am forever in your debt.

My deepest thanks also goes to the closest of friends I could have hoped for, Ryunosuke Ahsan (Ryu), my room-mate, class-mate, colleague, workout partner, and fellow dreamer. There is nothing as valuable as having a true friend that pushes you in all fields of life and reminds you of your stupidity when needed. Ryu is one of the calmest, kindest, and most sincere people I have met. I am beyond lucky to have lived life with him for the past three years during our time at university and college. You, literally, changed my life. And I am your biggest fan.

I would also like to thank Jesse John Gagnon and Matus Rajsky for giving me comments on certain chapters of the manuscript. Our conversations about these issues are one of the reasons I like to wake up in the morning. My two dear friends, Seth MacGregor and Jesse John have been fellow fierce debaters and close friends ever since I came to Canada. They have pushed me to want to be smarter and more curious. I love you both and I am thankful for the many conversations we've shared that have made this book more comprehensive.

Alex Houlton, I am thankful for your generosity and encouraging words in the process of writing this book. You always give me a place to stay when visiting Oxford to regain inspiration for life. You have been a close friend to me through the years despite the miles that often separate us. I will cherish our friendship forever and hope to have many more deep conversations with you wherever we find ourselves in the world.

Friendships mold you into who you are. I would not be who I am without my Slovakian childhood friends, Tomas Jadron, Marek Kovacik, Nikol Palencikova, Naomi Surovcek, Ivona Sramova, Miska Sramova, Ester Bobulova, Timo Bobula, Timothy Mulder, Andrej Poliacik, Dominik Pall, Armin Kamhal, Tomas Belica, Samuel Trizna, Marek Brezina, Filip Horvat, and so many more. I am thankful for all of your kindness and companionship. I am lucky to have such friends. And, Marek, I will remember you to the end of my days. You left us too soon and deserved a life akin to your contagious smile, intellect, and courage. You are sincerely missed.

Thank you to my Canadian friends who have been close to me through the years. Thank you, Colin Allen, Kevin Kelly, Court Funk, Charis Ord, Bobbi-Jo Bornau-Stauffer, and Zaylee Pollard-Homister for being so kind and caring. I am lucky to have such encouraging and thoughtful people around me.

I have had countless mentors throughout my life who encouraged me to read and think. I thank Igor Conka, my first pastor, who in my early years taught me that biblical discussions can be fascinating and edifying. Milos Masarik brought me to my first seminary to see what studying theology is like when I was 16 and satisfied my curiosity with dozens of conversations about God. Milos, thank you for always making time for me despite your demanding schedule. Graham Leeder invited me into his home many Mondays for most of my formative years to discuss biblical concepts. The books you lent me and the encouragement you gave are among the reasons I could persist in my endeavors. Esther and Will Chan have taught me to continuously show up and be generous; They have been immensely kind to me and put up with my youthful exuberance for too long and I am grateful for their patience. Above all, I am eternally thankful to my parents for showing me the meaning of sacrifice and perseverance in the face of adversity.

There are too many people to thank that have inadvertently contributed to this book and my life through conversations. Hundreds of coffee dates, walks, and phone calls with all of you have made my life such a joy. I am sincerely grateful to all who I failed to mention.

Lastly, my gratitude to you, the reader, is unending. Thank you for paying attention to the words I wrote and the thoughts I've had, there is nothing more valuable for you to give me. I will not take it for granted. Thank you.

Notes

Introduction

1. FitzGerald, Frances. *The Evangelicals*. Simon & Schuster, 2017, p. 232.

2. Heath, Joseph. *Enlightenment 2.0*. Harper Perennial, 2014, p. 164.

3. Baggett, David, and Jerry L. Walls. *The Moral Argument*. Oxford University Press, 2019, pp. 34-5.

4. Heath, Joseph. *Enlightenment 2.0*. Harper Perennial, 2014, pp. 351-2.

Chapter 1

1. "Why Knowledge and Logic Are Political Dirty Words." Kakutani, Michiko. *The New York Times*, The New York Times, 11 Mar. 2008, www.nytimes.com/2008/03/11/books/11kaku.html.

2. Heath, Joseph. *Enlightenment 2.0*. Harper Perennial, 2014, p. 162.

3. "Why Knowledge and Logic Are Political Dirty Words." Kakutani, Michiko. *The New York Times*, The New York Times, 11 Mar. 2008, www.nytimes.com/2008/03/11/books/11kaku.html.

4. Kaufmann, Eric. *Whiteshift*. Abrams Press, 2019, p. 217.

5. Shermer, Michael. *The Moral Arc*. Henry Holt and Co., 2015, p. 150.

6. Dawkins, Richard. *The God Delusion*. Black Swan, 2016, pp. 23, 306, 308.

7. Barker, Dan. *Mere Morality*. Pitchstone Publishing, 2018, p. 22.

8. Williams, Peter. *C.S. Lewis vs The New Atheists*. Paternoster, 2013, pp. 54–55.

9. Piper, John. "Think: The Life of the Mind and the Love of God." Crossway, 2010, p. 121.

10. Grudem, A., Wayne. *Christian Ethics*. Crossway, 2018, p. 165.

11. Long, Stephen. *Christian Ethics a Very Short Introduction*. Oxford University Press, 2010, p. 13.

12. FitzGerald, Frances. *The Evangelicals*. Simon & Schuster, 2017, p. 439.

13. Mohler, Albert. *The Way the World Thinks - Albert Mohler*. *YouTube*, Truth Endures, 2010, www.youtube.com/watch?v=YdN4-lX48U4.

14. Ibid.,

15 - Jacoby, Susan. *Strange Gods*. Vintage Books, a Division of Penguin Random House LLC, 2017, p. 15.

16. Grudem, A., Wayne. *Christian Ethics*. Crossway, 2018, pp. 377-8.

17. Piper, John. "Think: The Life of the Mind and the Love of God." Crossway,

2010, p. 123.

18. Zacharias, K., Ravi, and Durant, Danielle. *Beyond Opinion*. Thomas Nelson, 2010, p. 53.

19. Ibid., 53.

Chapter 2

1. Zuckerman, Paul. *Living the Secular Life*. Penguin Press, 2014, p. 5.

2. Ibid., 58.

3. Ibid., 20-1.

4. Ibid., 20-1.

5. Ibid., 21.

6. Gottlieb, Anthony. *The Dream of Reason*. Penguin, 2016, p. 137.

7. Ibid., 21.

8. Ibid., 21.

9. Ibid., 224.

10. Grayling, C. Anthony. *The History of Philosophy*. Penguin Press, 2019, p. 67.

11. Ibid., 68.

12. Ibid., 68.

13. Gottlieb, Anthony. *The Dream of Reason*. Penguin, 2016, p. 391.

14. Grayling, C. Anthony. *The History of Philosophy*. Penguin Press, 2019, p. 154.

15. Gottlieb, Anthony. *The Dream of Reason*. Penguin, 2016, p. 363.

16. Ibid., 281.

17. Ibid., 363.

18. Ibid., 231.

19. Ibid., 231.

20. Ibid., 231.

21. Ibid., 237.

22. Ibid., 363.

23. Ibid., 363.

24. Ibid., 363.

25. Ibid., 427.

26. Malik, Kenan. *The Quest for a Moral Compass*. Atlantic Books, 2015, p. 164.

27. Grayling, C. Anthony. *The History of Philosophy*. Penguin Press, 2019, p. 184.

28. Ibid., 199.

29. Foucault, Michel. *The Order of Things*. Vintage Books, 1994, p. 5.

30. Ibid., 14.

31. Ibid., 16.

32. Gottlieb, Anthony. *The Dream of Enlightenment*. Liverlight, 2017, p. 92.

33. Malik, Kenan. *The Quest for a Moral Compass*. Atlantic Books, 2015, p. 186.

34. Gottlieb, Anthony. *The Dream of Enlightenment*. Liverlight, 2017, p. 98.

35. Ibid., 111.

36. Ibid., 156.

37. Ibid., 223.

38. Malik, Kenan. *The Quest for a Moral Compass.* Atlantic Books, 2015, p. 170.

39. Ibid., 171.

40. Ibid., 179.

41. Schwitzbegel, E., and J. Rust. 2009. "Do Ethicists and Political Philosophers Vote More Often than Other Professors?" *Review of Philosophy and Psychology* 1:189-99 --.2011. "The Self-Reported Moral Behavior of Ethics Professors." Unpublished ms., University of California at Riverside.

42. Duffy, Bobby. *Why We're Wrong About Nearly Everything.* Basic Books, 2019, p. 3.

43. Ibid., pp. 3-4.

44. Dawkins, Richard, and Dave McKean. *The Magic of Reality.* Black Swan, 2012, p. 15.

45. Watson, Peter. *The Age of Atheists.* Simon & Schuster, 2014, p. 528.

46. Stanovich, Keith E. *The Robot's Rebellion.* University of Chicago Press, 2004, p. 163.

47. Heath, Joseph. *Enlightenment 2.0.* Harper Perennial, 2014, p. 137.

48. Ibid., 104.

49. Ibid., 231.

50. Ibid., 232.

51. Ibid., 138.

52. Ibid., 139.

53. Ibid., 137.

54. Ibid., 162.

55. Ibid., 105.

56. Haidt, Jonathan. *The Righteous Mind.* Vintage Books, 2013, p. 103.

57. Ibid., 103.

58. Heath, Joseph. *Enlightenment 2.0.* Harper Perennial, 2014, p. 192.

59. Ibid., 211.

60. Ibid., 212.

Chapter 3

1. Malik, Kenan. *The Quest for a Moral Compass.* Atlantic Books, 2015, p. 58.

2. Grudem, A., Wayne. *Christian Ethics.* Crossway, 2018, p. 30.

3. Shermer, Michael. *The Moral Arc.* Henry Holt and Co., 2015, p. 154.

4. "Why Are You so Afraid of Subjective Moral Reasoning?" *YouTube,* Ravi Zacharias International Ministries, 2014, www.youtube.com/watch?v=0218GkAGbnU.

5. Keller, Timothy. *Making Sense of God.* Hodder & Stoughton Ltd, 2018, p. 178.

6. Lennox, John C. *Gunning for God.* Lion, 2011, p. 101.

7. Grudem, A., Wayne. *Christian Ethics.* Crossway, 2018, p. 86.

8. Keller, Timothy. *Making Sense of God.* Hodder & Stoughton Ltd, 2018, p. 186.

9. Grayling, C., Anthony. *The God Argument*. Bloomsbury Publishing, 2013, p. 189.

10. Dawkins, Richard. *Outgrowing God*. Random House, 2019, p. 102.

11. Zacharias, K., Ravi, and Durant, Danielle. *Beyond Opinion*. Thomas Nelson, 2010, p. 54.

12. Ibid., 54.

13. Ibid., 55.

14. Grudem, A., Wayne. *Christian Ethics*. Crossway, 2018, p. 707.

15. Ley, David J. *Ethical Porn for Dicks*. ThreeL Media, 2016, p. 93.

16. "Homosexuality and the Campaign for Immorality (Selected Scriptures)." *YouTube*, Grace to You, 2012, www.youtube.com/watch?v=hOGqVyYYfHc.

17. Ibid.

18. "The Meaning of Marriage | Timothy Keller | Talks at Google." *YouTube*, Talks at Google, 2011, www.youtube.com/watch?v=C9THuOPZwwk.

19. Wright, Robert. *The Evolution of God*. Abacus, 2013, p. 316.

20. Ibid., 316.

21. Grudem, A., Wayne. *Christian Ethics*. Crossway, 2018, p. 739.

22. "John MacArthur | The Ben Shapiro Show Sunday Special Ep. 29." *YouTube*, Ben Shapiro, 2018, www.youtube.com/watch?v=ak-Rv08N_1Q.

23. Greene, Joshua. *Moral Tribes*. Atlantic Books, 2015, pp. 180-1.

24. Grudem, A., Wayne. *Christian Ethics*. Crossway, 2018, p. 88.

Chapter 4

1. Pinker, Steven. *The Better Angels of Our Nature*. Viking, 2011, p. 6.

2. Russell, Bertrand. *Why I am Not a Christian*. Simon & Schuster, inc. 1957, p. 25.

3. "Yuval Noah Harari & Natalie Portman." *YouTube*, How to Academy, 2018, https://www.youtube.com/watch?v=87XFTJXH9sc.

4. Churchland, Patricia Smith. *Braintrust*. Princeton University Press, 2018, p. 165.

5. Gray, John. "Moral Tribes: Emotion, Reason, and the Gap Between Us and Them by Joshua Greene – Review." *The Guardian*, Guardian News and Media, 17 Jan. 2014, www.theguardian.com/books/2014/jan/17/moral-tribes-joshua-greene-review.

6. Shermer, Michael. *The Moral Arc*. Henry Holt and Co., 2015, p. 11.

7. Churchland, Patricia Smith. *Braintrust*. Princeton University Press, 2018, p. 166.

8. Keller, Timothy. *Making Sense of God*. Hodder & Stoughton Ltd, 2018, p. 185.

9. Lennox, John C. *Gunning for God*. Lion, 2011, p. 98.

10. Churchland, Patricia Smith. *Braintrust*. Princeton University Press, 2018, 199.

11. Shermer, Michael. *The Moral Arc*. Henry Holt and Co., 2015, p. 169.

12. Ibid., 169.
13. Zuckerman, Phil. *Living the Secular Life*. Penguin Press, 2014, p. 46.
14. Dawkins, Richard. *The God Delusion*. Black Swan, 2016, p. 262.
15. Long, Stephen. *Christian Ethics*. Oxford University Press, 2010, p. 68.
16. Keller, Timothy. *Making Sense of God*. Hodder & Stoughton Ltd, 2018, p. 182.
17. Levitin, Daniel J. *The Organized Mind*. Dutton an Imprint of Penguin Random House, 2017, p. 196.
18. Christakis, Nicholas A. *Blueprint*. Little, Brown Spark, 2020, pp. 180-1.
19. Dawkins, Richard. *The God Delusion*. Black Swan, 2016, p. 247.
20. Ibid., 252.
21. Ibid., 252.
22. Ibid., 253.
23. Ibid., 253.
24. Churchland, Patricia Smith. *Braintrust*. Princeton University Press, 2018, p. 64.
25. Ibid., 64.
26. Christakis, Nicholas A. *Blueprint*. Little, Brown Spark, 2020, p. 284.
27. Ibid., 284.
28. Churchland, Patricia Smith. *Braintrust*. Princeton University Press, 2018, pp. 70-1.
29. Harari Yuval Noah. *Homo Deus*. Harper Perennial, 2018, p. 95.
30. Keller, Timothy. *Making Sense of God*. Hodder & Stoughton Ltd, 2018, p. 183.
31. Ibid., 183.
32. Churchland, Patricia Smith. *Braintrust*. Princeton University Press, 2018, p. 27.
33. Ibid., 30.
34. Harari Yuval Noah. *Homo Deus*. Harper Perennial, 2018, p. 102.
35. Heath, Joseph. *Enlightenment 2.0*. Harper Perennial, 2014, p. 106.
36. Grayling, C., Anthony. *The God Argument*. Bloomsbury Publishing, 2013, p. 141.
37. Churchland, Patricia Smith. *Braintrust*. Princeton University Press, 2018, p. 201.
38. Harris, Sam. *The Moral Landscape*. Free Press, 2010, p. 57.
39. Epstein, Greg M. *Good without God: What a Billion Nonreligious People Do Believe*. Harper, 2010, pp. 146-7.
40. MacAskill, William. *Doing Good Better*. Faber & Faber, 2016, p. 99.
41. Singer, Peter. *The Most Good You Can Do*. The Text Publishing Company, 2016, p. 75.
42. Harari Yuval Noah. *Homo Deus*. Harper Perennial, 2018, p. 6.

43. Pinker, Steven. *The Better Angels of Our Nature*. Viking, 2011, p. 10.

44. Ibid., 10.

45. Ibid., 10.

46. Ibid., 10.

47. Ibid., 8.

48. Frame, John M. *Nature's Case for God*. Lexham Press, 2018, p. 79.

49. Barker, Dan. *Mere Morality.*, Pitchstone Publishing, 2018, pp. 99-100.

50. Grayling, C., Anthony. *The God Argument*. Bloomsbury Publishing, 2013, p. 241.

51. Ibid., 240.

52. Ibid., 238.

53. Barker, Dan. *Mere Morality*. Pitchstone Publishing, 2018, p. 127.

Chapter 5

1. "Tuesday, August 11, 2020." Mohler, Albert. *Albertmohler.com*, 2020, albert-mohler.com/2020/08/11/briefing-8-11-20?fbclid=IwAR3eOQIbYlcUK8 DAYdNsX6tYjY4BeTI89i8zMG3EGrs4q2QJ94ZdXr0bmF4.

2. Watson, Peter. *The Age of Atheists*. Simon & Schuster, 2014, 309.

3. Ibid., 309.

4. Long, Stephen. *Christian Ethics: A Very Short Introduction*. Oxford University Press, 2010, p. 60.

5. Wright, Robert. *The Evolution of God*. Abacus, 2013, p. 305.

6. Grudem, A., Wayne. *Christian Ethics*. Crossway, 2018, p. 475.

7. Jacoby, Susan. *Strange Gods*. Vintage Books, a Division of Penguin Random House LLC, 2017, pp. 144-5.

8. FitzGerald, Frances. *The Evangelicals*. Simon & Schuster, 2017, p. 3.

9. Ibid., 3.

10. Ibid., 4.

11. Ibid., 7.

12. Ibid., 636.

13. Ibid., 143.

14. Ibid., 184.

15. Ibid., pp. 184-5.

16. Ibid., 289.

17. Ibid., 292.

18. Ibid., 292.

19. Ibid., 292.

20. Ibid., 367.

21. Ibid., 420.

22. Ibid., 267.

23. Ibid., 433.

24. Ibid., 464.

25. Ibid., 464.

26. Kaufmann, Eric. *Whiteshif.* Abrams Press, 2019, p. 85.

27. FitzGerald, Frances. *The Evangelicals.* Simon & Schuster, 2017, p. 534.

28. Kaufmann, Eric. *Whiteshif.* Abrams Press, 2019, p. 87.

29. Ibid., 87.

30. Ibid., 87.

31. FitzGerald, Frances. *The Evangelicals.* Simon & Schuster, 2017, p. 536.

32. Ibid., 539.

33. Ibid., 539-40.

34. Ibid., 610.

35. Ibid., 610.

36. Ibid., 610.

37. Ibid., 619.

38. Ibid., 619.

39. Ibid., 535.

40. Zmirak, John. "Systemic Racism and Other Conspiracy Theories." *The Stream,* 11 June 2020, stream.org/systemic-racism-and-other-conspiracy-theories/.

41. Duffy, Bobby. *Why We're Wrong About Nearly Everything.* Basic Books, 2019, p. 58.

42. Ibid., 58.

43. Ibid., 58.

44. "Abortions Worldwide This Year:" *Worldometer,* 2020, www.worldometers.info/abortions/.

45. FitzGerald, Frances. *The Evangelicals.* Simon & Schuster, 2017, p. 610.

46. Grudem, A., Wayne. *Christian Ethics.* Crossway, 2018, pp. 409-10.

47. Ibid., 409-10.

48. Ibid., 410.

49. "10 Reasons God Loves Gay Christians." Vines, Matthew. *Time,* 11 June 2014, time.com/2842044/gay-christians/.

50. Kaufmann, Eric. *Whiteshif.* Abrams Press, 2019, p. 87.

51. Haidt, Jonathan. *The Happiness Hypothesis.* Cornerstone Digital, 2015, p. 242.

52. Grudem, A., Wayne. *Christian Ethics.* Crossway, 2018, p. 476.

53. Ibid., 476.

54. Shermer, Michael. *The Moral Arc.* Henry Holt and Co., 2015, p. 203.

55. Grudem, A., Wayne. *Christian Ethics.* Crossway, 2018, p. 476.

56. Harris, Murray J. *Slave of Christ.* Apollos, 2001, p. 44.

57. Wallace-Wells, David. *The Uninhabitable Earth.* Tim Duggan Books, 2019, p. 133.

58. Ibid., 133.

59. Ibid., 133.

60. Kaufmann, Eric. *Whiteshift*. Abrams Press, 2019, p. 260.

61. Ibid., 212.

62. Ibid., 218.

63. Ibid., 215.

64. "Brazil's President Bolsonaro on Socialism, Trade and Trump." *YouTube*, Fox News, 2019, www.youtube.com/watch?v=6VSEp5tf7lg.

65. Kaufmann, Eric. *Whiteshift*. Abrams Press, 2019, p. 219.

66. "Hungary's Orban Warns Economic Migration Endangers Europeans." *YouTube*, Euronews, 2015, www.youtube.com/watch?v=v6KdA5Y87PE.

67. Kaufmann, Eric. *Whiteshift*. Abrams Press, 2019, p. 247.

68. United Nations High Commissioner for Refugees. "Figures at a Glance." *UNHCR*, 2019, www.unhcr.org/figures-at-a-glance.html.

69. Kaufmann, Eric. *Whiteshift*. Abrams Press, 2019, p. 234.

70. Ibid., 234.

71. Ibid., 236.

72. Ibid., 236.

73. FitzGerald, Frances. *The Evangelicals*. Simon & Schuster, 2017, p. 547.

74. Ibid., 550.

75. Ibid., 550.

Chapter 6

1. Harari Yuval Noah. *Homo Deus*. Harper Perennial, 2018, p. 313.

2. Malik, Kenan. *The Quest for a Moral Compass*. Atlantic Books, 2015, p. 75.

3. Heath, Joseph. *Enlightenment 2.0*. Harper Perennial, 2014, p. 253.

4. Pinker, Steven. *The Better Angels of Our Nature*. Viking, 2011, p. 133.

5. Ibid., 149.

6. Ibid., 149.

7. Ibid., 149.

8. Wright, Robert. *The Evolution of God*. Abacus, 2013, p. 280.

9. Ibid., 280.

10. Ibid., 281.

11. Shermer, Michael. *The Moral Arc*. Henry Holt and Co., 2015, p. 151.

12. Ibid., 152.

13. Wright, Robert. *The Evolution of God*. Abacus, 2013, p. 283.

14. Jacoby, Susan. *Strange Gods*. Vintage Books, a Division of Penguin Random House LLC, 2017, pp. 412-3.

15. Harari, Yuval N. *Sapiens*. Harper Perennial, 2018, p. 216.

16. Nicholls, William. *Christian Antisemitism*. Rowman & Littlefield Pub., 2004, p. 182.

17. Grayling, A. C. *Towards the Light*. Bloomsbury Academic, 2014, p. 28.

18. Pinker, Steven. *The Better Angels of Our Nature*. Viking, 2011, p. 231.

19. Ibid., 231.
20. Shermer, Michael. *The Moral Arc*. Henry Holt and Co., 2015, p. 150.
21. Pinker, Steven. *The Better Angels of Our Nature*. Viking, 2011, p. 140.
22. Ibid., 140.
23. Jacoby, Susan. *Strange Gods*. Vintage Books, a Division of Penguin Random House LLC, 2017, p. 15.
24. Grayling, A. C. *Towards the Light*. Bloomsbury Academic, 2014, p. 24.
25. Jacoby, Susan. *Strange Gods*. Vintage Books, a Division of Penguin Random House LLC, 2017, p. 151.
26. Ibid., 151.
27. Ibid., 150.
28. Pinker, Steven. *The Better Angels of Our Nature*. Viking, 2011, p. 142.
29. Jacoby, Susan. *Strange Gods*. Vintage Books, a Division of Penguin Random House LLC, 2017, pp. 144-5.
30. Pinker, Steven. *The Better Angels of Our Nature*. Viking, 2011, p. 141.
31. Grayling, A. C. *Towards the Light*. Bloomsbury Academic, 2014, p. 35.
32. Ibid., 52.
33. Ibid., 48.
34. Martin, Robert M., and Andrew Bailey. *First Philosophy*. Broadview Press, 2012, p. 47.
35. Grayling, A. C. *Towards the Light*. Bloomsbury Academic, 2014, p. 63.
36. Ibid., 75.
37. Ibid., 74.
38. Jacoby, Susan. *Strange Gods*. Vintage Books, a Division of Penguin Random House LLC, 2017, p. 186.
39. Nicholls, William. *Christian Antisemitism*. Rowman & Littlefield Pub., 2004, pp. 269-70.
40. Ibid., 270.
41. Pinker, Steven. *The Better Angels of Our Nature*. Viking, 2011, p. 143.
42. Nicholls, William. *Christian Antisemitism*. Rowman & Littlefield Pub., 2004, p. 274.
43. Ibid., 272.
44. Grayling, A. C. *Towards the Light*. Bloomsbury Academic, 2014, p. 1.
45. Fukuyama, Francis. *The Origins of Political Order*. Farrar, Straus and Giroux, 2011, p. 328.
46. Ibid., 328.
47. Ibid., 329.
48. Ibid., pp. 329-30.
49. Ibid., 330.
50. Ibid., 329.
51. Pinker, Steven. *The Better Angels of Our Nature*. Viking, 2011, p. 149.

52. Grayling, A. C. *Towards the Light*. Bloomsbury Academic, 2014, p. 134.

53. Ibid., 134.

54. Clapham, Andrew. *Human Rights*. Oxford University Press, 2015, p. 5.

55. Ibid., 6.

56. "Jean Jacques Rousseau." Bertram, Christopher. *Stanford Encyclopedia of Philosophy*, Stanford University, 26 May 2017, plato.stanford.edu/entries/rousseau/.

57. Grayling, C., Anthony. *The History of Philosophy*. Penguin Press, 2019, p. 270.

58. Ibid., 270.

59. Stewart, Robert M. *Readings in Social and Political Philosophy*. Oxford University Press, 1996, p. 49.

60. Clapham, Andrew. *Human Rights*. Oxford University Press, 2015, p. 13.

61. Watson, Peter. *The Age of Atheists*. Simon & Schuster, 2014, p. 503.

62. Clapham, Andrew. *Human Rights*. Oxford University Press, 2015, p. 17.

63. Watson, Peter. *The Age of Atheists*. Simon & Schuster, 2014, p. 534.

64. Clapham, Andrew. *Human Rights*. Oxford University Press, 2015, p. 27.

65. See: "The Case against Human Rights | Eric Posner." Posner, Eric. *The Guardian*, Guardian News and Media, 4 Dec. 2014, www.theguardian.com/news/2014/dec/04/-sp-case-against-human-rights.

66. Harari, Yuval Noah. *Sapiens*. Harper Perennial, 2018, p. 145.

67. Watson, Peter. *The Age of Atheists*. Simon & Schuster, 2014, p. 368.

68. Ibid., 367.

69. Pinker, Steven. *The Better Angels of Our Nature*. Viking, 2011, p. 449.

70. Russell, Bertrand. *Why I am Not a Christian*. Simon & Schuster, inc. 1957, p. 27.

71. Pinker, Steven. *The Better Angels of Our Nature*. Viking, 2011, p. 137.

72. Ibid., 138.

73. Ibid., 139.

74. Singer, Peter. *Ethics in the Real World*. Princeton University Press, 2016, p. 18.

75. Shermer, Michael. *The Moral Arc*. Henry Holt and Co., 2015, p. 253.

76. Pinker, Steven. *The Better Angels of Our Nature*. Viking, 2011, p. 177.

77. Ibid., 177.

78. Ibid., 177.

79. Ibid., 589.

80. Ibid., 179.

81. Ibid., 179.

82. Malik, Kenan. *The Quest for a Moral Compass*. Atlantic Books, 2015, p. 334.

Chapter 7

1. Schaeffer, Francis August. *Pollution and the Death of Man*. Tyndale House

Publishers, 1981, p. 78.

2. Wallace-Wells, David. *The Uninhabitable Earth*. Tim Duggan Books, 2019, p. 166.

3. Ibid., 166.

4. Ibid., 14.

5. Ibid., 183.

6. Ibid., 119.

7. Ibid., 69.

8. Ibid., 64.

9. Ibid., 119.

10. Ibid., 68.

11. Grudem, A., Wayne. *Christian Ethics*. Crossway, 2018, p. 1106.

12. Schaeffer, Francis August. *Pollution and the Death of Man*. Tyndale House Publishers, 1981, pp. 108-9.

13. Ibid., 39.

14. Ibid., 39.

15. Ibid., 41.

16. Ibid., 77.

17. Reese, Jacy. *The End of Animal Farming*. Beacon Press, 2019, p. 3.

18. Pinker, Steven. *The Better Angels of Our Nature*. Viking, 2011, p. 148.

19. Ibid., 148.

20. Ibid., 466.

21. Castaldo, Nancy F. *Beastly Brains*. Houghton Mifflin Harcourt, 2017, p. 116.

22. Smith, Wesley J. *A Rat Is a Pig Is a Dog Is a Boy*. Encounter Books, 2012, p. 2.

23. Ibid., 3.

24. Ibid., 242.

25. Ibid., 242.

26. Christakis, Nicholas A. *Blueprint*. Little, Brown Spark, 2020, p. 331.

27. Ibid., 393.

28. Grudem, A., Wayne. *Christian Ethics*. Crossway, 2018, p. 1101.

29. Marks, Jonathan M. *What It Means to Be 98% Chimpanzee*. Univ. of California Press, 2005, p. 188.

30. Ibid., 191.

31. Ibid., 187.

32. Ibid., 191.

33. Ibid., 23.

34. Ibid., 31.

35. Shanor, Karen, and Jagmeet S. Kanwal. *Bats Sing Mice Giggle*. Icon, 2010, p. 157.

36. Ibid., 59.

37. Ibid., 102.

38. Castaldo, Nancy F. *Beastly Brains*. Houghton Mifflin Harcourt, 2017, p. 66.

39. Christakis, Nicholas A. *Blueprint*. Little, Brown Spark, 2020, p. 218.

40. Reese, Jacy. *The End of Animal Farming*. Beacon Press, 2019, p. 7.

41. Ibid., 7.

42. Christakis, Nicholas A. *Blueprint*. Little, Brown Spark, 2020, p. 283.

43. Harris, Annaka. *Conscious*. Harper, 2019, p. 5.

44. Shermer, Michael. *The Moral Arc*. Henry Holt and Co., 2015, p. 12.

45. Reese, Jacy. *The End of Animal Farming*. Beacon Press, 2019, p. 9.

46. Wallace-Wells, David. *The Uninhabitable Earth*. Tim Duggan Books, 2019, p. 49.

47. "Industrial Farming Is One of the Worst Crimes in History." Harari, Yuval Noah. *The Guardian*, Guardian News and Media, 25 Sept. 2015, www.theguardian.com/books/2015/sep/25/industrial-farming-one-worst-crimes-history-ethical-question.

48. "How Many Animals Are Killed for Food Every Day?" Zampa, Matt. *Reporting on Animals, Animal Rights, and Human Choices*, 4 Aug. 2020, sentient-media.org/how-many-animals-are-killed-for-food-every-day/.

49. "Antibiotics and the Meat We Eat." Kessler, David A. *The New York Times*, The New York Times, 28 Mar. 2013, www.nytimes.com/2013/03/28/opinion/antibiotics-and-the-meat-we-eat.html.

50. McCarthy, Matt. *Superbugs*. Scribe Publications, 2019, p. 118.

51. Ibid., 118.

52. "We Have to Wake up: Factory Farms Are Breeding Grounds for Pandemics | Jonathan Safran Foer and Aaron S Gross." Foer, Jonathan Safran, and Aaron S Gross. *The Guardian*, Guardian News and Media, 20 Apr. 2020, www.theguardian.com/commentisfree/2020/apr/20/factory-farms-pandemic-risk-covid-animal-human-health.

53. See: Reese, Jacy. *The End of Animal Farming*. Beacon Press, 2019.

54. Metaxas, Eric. *Martin Luther*. Penguin Books, 2018, p. 11.

55. Grudem, A., Wayne. *Christian Ethics*. Crossway, 2018, p. 1105.

56. Harari, Yuval Noah. *Sapiens: A Brief History of Humankind*. Harper Perennial, 2014. 107.

Chapter 8

1. Singer, Peter. *The Most Good You Can Do*. The Text Publishing Company, 2016, p. 177.

2. MacAskill, William. *Doing Good Better*. Faber & Faber, 2016, p. 95.

3. Ibid., 95.

4. Ibid., 95.

5. Wallace-Wells, David. *The Uninhabitable Earth*. Tim Duggan Books, 2019, p. 27.

6. MacAskill, William. *Doing Good Better*. Faber & Faber, 2016, p. 96.

7. Wallace-Wells, David. *The Uninhabitable Earth*. Tim Duggan Books, 2019, p. 183.

8. Ibid., 75.

9. "Peter Singer: On Racism, Animal Rights and Human Rights." Yancy, George. *The New York Times*, 2015, opinionator.blogs.nytimes.com/2015/05/27/peter-singer-on-speciesism-and-racism/.

10. Ibid.

11. Malik, Kenan. *The Quest for a Moral Compass*. Atlantic Books, 2015, p. 213.

12. Greene, Joshua. *Moral Tribes*. Atlantic Books, 2015, p. 349.

13. Ibid., pp. 203-4.

14. Not Peter Singer's argument, quoting someone called Ian. Singer, Peter. *The Most Good You Can Do*. The Text Publishing Company, 2016, p. 44.

Chapter 9

1. Watson, Peter. *The Age of Atheists*. Simon & Schuster, 2014, p. 307.

2. Grudem, A., Wayne. *Christian Ethics*. Crossway, 2018, p. 539.

3. Bostrom, Nick, and Ćirković Milan M. *Global Catastrophic Risks*. Oxford University Press, 2008, p. 386.

4. Ibid., 386.

5. Ibid., 386.

6. Ibid., 386.

7. Ibid., 386.

8. Ibid., 390.

9. Ibid., 390.

10. Ibid., 390.

11. Grudem, A., Wayne. *Christian Ethics*. Crossway, 2018, p. 528.

12. Ibid., pp. 529-30.

13. Ibid., 539.

Chapter 10

1. Bostrom, Nick, and Ćirković Milan M. *Global Catastrophic Risks*. Oxford University Press, 2008, p. 382.

2. Ibid., 382.

3. Ibid., 381.

4. Ibid., 383.

5. Perry, William James, and Tom Z. Collina. *The Button*. BenBella Books, Inc., 2020, p. 43.

6. "Keep Nuclear Testing off the Table - The Boston Globe." T. Klare, Michael, and Daryl G. Kimball. *BostonGlobe.com*, The Boston Globe, 13 June 2020, www.bostonglobe.com/2020/06/13/opinion/keep-nuclear-testing-off-table/?fbclid=IwAR0rJQ1W4BETXQ7_Sf7ECf4qw6RCDxhSN73mKzW1jQBpg5bWva_AjU5Z3J8.

7. "Comprehensive Test Ban Treaty at a Glance." Kimball, Daryl. *Arms Control Association*, July 2020, www.armscontrol.org/factsheets/test-ban-treaty-at-a-glance.

8. Bostrom, Nick, and Ćirković Milan M. *Global Catastrophic Risks*. Oxford University Press, 2008, p. 383.

9. Ibid., pp. 383-4.

10. Ibid., 388.

11. Ibid., 389.

12. Ibid., 389.

13. Perry, William James, and Tom Z. Collina. *The Button*. BenBella Books, Inc., 2020, p. 91.

14. Pinker, Steven. *Enlightenment Now: The Case for Reason, Science, Humanism, and Progress*. Penguin Books, 2019, p. 291.

15. Perry, William James, and Tom Z. Collina. *The Button*. BenBella Books, Inc., 2020, p. 50.

16. Ord, Toby. *The Precipice*. Bloomsbury, 2020, p. 96.

17. Ibid., 97.

18. Ibid., 97.

19. Ibid., 265.

20. Ibid., 266

21. Perry, William James, and Tom Z. Collina. *The Button*. BenBella Books, Inc., 2020, p. 99.

22. Ibid., 9.

Chapter 11

1. Colson, Charles Wendell, and Harold Fickett. *The Good Life*. Tyndale House Publishers, 2006, p. 100.

2. Keller, Timothy. *Making Sense of God*. Hodder & Stoughton Ltd, 2018, p. 163.

3. Ibid., pp. 166-7.

4. Colson, Charles Wendell, and Harold Fickett. *The Good Life*. Tyndale House Publishers, 2006, p. 112.

5. Ibid., 241.

6. Ehrman, Bart D. *Triumph of Christianity*. Simon & Schuster. 2018, p. 153.

7. Ibid., 154.

8. Ibid., 153.

9. Ibid., 154.

10. Ibid., 92.

11. Nicholls, William. *Christian Antisemitism*. Rowman & Littlefield Pub., 2004, p. 240.

12. Ibid., 241.

13. Ibid., 241.

Chapter 12

1. Camus, Albert. *The Myth of Sisyphus*. Vintage International, 2018, p. 119.
2. Haidt, Jonathan. *The Happiness Hypothesis*. Cornerstone Digital, 2015, p. 133.
3. Ibid., 76.
4. Ibid., 86.
5. Ibid., 85.
6. Ibid., 86.
7. Ibid., 88.
8. Ibid., pp. 132-3.
9. Ibid., p. 133.
10. Ibid., 151.
11. Harris, Sam. *Waking Up*. Simon Schuster, 2015, p. 12.
12. Ibid., 47.
13. Ibid., 83.
14. Ibid., 100.
15. Haidt, Jonathan. *The Happiness Hypothesis*. Cornerstone Digital, 2015, p. 87.
16. Shermer, Michael. *The Moral Arc*. Henry Holt and Co., 2015, p. 439.

Bibliography

"Abortions Worldwide This Year:" *Worldometer*, 2020, www.worldometers.info/abortions/.

"Antibiotics and the Meat We Eat." Kessler, David A. *The New York Times*, The New York Times, 28 Mar. 2013, www.nytimes.com/2013/03/28/opinion/antibiotics-and-the-meat-we-eat.html.

Baggett, David, and Jerry L. Walls. *The Moral Argument: A History*. Oxford University Press, 2019.

Barker, Dan. *Mere Morality*. Pitchstone Publishing, 2018.

"Brazil's President Bolsonaro on Socialism, Trade and Trump." *YouTube*, Fox News, 2019, www.youtube.com/watch?v=6VSEp5tf7lg.

Bostrom, Nick, and Ćirković Milan M. *Global Catastrophic Risks*. Oxford University Press, 2008.

Camus, Albert. *The Myth of Sisyphus*. Vintage International, 2018.

Castaldo, Nancy F. *Beastly Brains: Exploring How Animals Talk, Think, and Feel*. Houghton Mifflin Harcourt, 2017.

Christakis, Nicholas A. *Blueprint: The Evolutionary Origins of a Good Society*. Little, Brown Spark, 2020.

Churchland, Patricia Smith. *Braintrust: What Neuroscience Tells Us about Morality*. Princeton University Press, 2018.

Clapham, Andrew. *Human Rights: A Very Short Introduction*. Oxford University Press, 2015.

Colson, Charles Wendell, and Harold Fickett. *The Good Life*. Tyndale House Publishers, 2006.

"Comprehensive Test Ban Treaty at a Glance." Kimball, Daryl. *Arms Control*

Association, July 2020, www.armscontrol.org/factsheets/test-ban-treaty-at-a-glance.

Dawkins, Richard. *The God Delusion*. Black Swan, 2016.

Dawkins, Richard. *Outgrowing God: A Beginner's Guide to Atheism*. Random House, 2019.

Dawkins, Richard, and Dave McKean. *The Magic of Reality: How We Know What's Really True*. Black Swan, 2012.

Duffy, Bobby. *Why We're Wrong About Nearly Everything: A Theory of Human Misunderstanding*. Basic Books, 2019.

Epstein, Greg M. *Good without God: What a Billion Nonreligious People Do Believe*. Harper, 2010

Ehrman, Bart D. *Triumph of Christianity: How a Forbidden Religion Swept the World*. Simon & Schuster. 2018.

FitzGerald, Frances. *The Evangelicals: The Struggle to Shape America*. Simon & Schuster, 2017.

Foucault, Michel. *The Order of Things: An Archaeology of the Human Sciences*. Vintage Books, 1994.

Frame, John M. *Nature's Case for God: A Brief Biblical Argument*. Lexham Press, 2018.

Fukuyama, Francis. *The Origins of Political Order*. Farrar, Straus and Giroux, 2011.

Gottlieb, Anthony. *The Dream of Enlightenment: The Rise of Modern Philosophy*. Liverlight, 2017.

Gottlieb, Anthony. *The Dream of Reason: A History of Western Philosophy from the Greeks to the Renaissance*. Penguin, 2016.

Greene, Joshua. *Moral Tribes: Emotion, Reason, and the Gap between Us and Them*. Atlantic Books, 2015.

Grayling, C., Anthony. *The God Argument: The Case against Religion and for Humanism*. Bloomsbury Publishing, 2013.

Grayling, C., Anthony. *The History of Philosophy*. Penguin Press, 2019.

Grayling, A. C. *Towards the Light: The Story of the Struggles for Liberty and Rights*

That Made the Modern West. Bloomsbury Academic, 2014.

Grudem, A., Wayne. *Christian Ethics: An Introduction to Biblical Moral Reasoning.* Crossway, 2018.

Haidt, Jonathan. *The Happiness Hypothesis: Putting Ancient Wisdom to the Test of Modern Science.* Cornerstone Digital, 2015.

Haidt, Jonathan. *The Righteous Mind: Why Good People Are Divided by Politics and Religion.* Vintage Books, 2013.

Harari Yuval Noaḥ. *Homo Deus: A Brief History of Tomorrow.* Harper Perennial, 2018.

Harari, Yuval Noah. *Sapiens: A Brief History of Humankind.* Harper Perennial, 2014.

Harris, Annaka. *Conscious: A Brief Guide to the Fundamental Mystery of the Mind.* Harper, 2019.

Harris, Murray J. *Slave of Christ: a New Testament Metaphor for Total Devotion to Christ.* Apollos, 2001.

Harris, Sam. *The Moral Landscape: How Science Can Determine Human Values.* Free Press, 2010.

Harris, Sam. *Waking Up: A Guide to Spirituality Without Religion.* Simon Schuster, 2015.

Heath, Joseph. *Enlightenment 2.0: Restoring Sanity to Our Politics.* Harper Perennial, 2014.

"Homosexuality and the Campaign for Immorality (Selected Scriptures)." *YouTube,* Grace to You, 2012, www.youtube.com/watch?v=h0GqVyYYfHc.

"How Many Animals Are Killed for Food Every Day?" Zampa, Matt. *Reporting on Animals, Animal Rights, and Human Choices,* 4 Aug. 2020, sentientmedia.org/how-many-animals-are-killed-for-food-every-day/.

"Hungary's Orban Warns Economic Migration Endangers Europeans." *YouTube,* Euronews, 2015, www.youtube.com/watch?v=v6KdA5Y87PE.

"Industrial Farming Is One of the Worst Crimes in History." Harari, Yuval Noah. *The Guardian,* Guardian News and Media, 25 Sept. 2015, www.theguardian.com/books/2015/sep/25/industrial-farming-one-worst-crimes-history-ethical-question.

Jacoby, Susan. *Strange Gods: A Secular History of Conversion.* Vintage Books, a Division of Penguin Random House LLC, 2017.

"Jean Jacques Rousseau." Bertram, Christopher. *Stanford Encyclopedia of Philosophy*, Stanford University, 26 May 2017, plato.stanford.edu/entries/rousseau/.

Kaufmann, Eric. *Whiteshift: Populism, Immigration and the Future of White Majorities.* Abrams Press, 2019.

"Keep Nuclear Testing off the Table - The Boston Globe." T. Klare, Michael, and Daryl G. Kimball. *BostonGlobe.com*, The Boston Globe, 13 June 2020, www.bostonglobe.com/2020/06/13/opinion/keep-nuclear-testing-off-table/?fbclid=IwAR0rJQ1W4BETXQ7_Sf7ECf4qw6RCDxhSN73mKzW1jQBpg5b-Wva_AjU5Z3J8.

Keller, Timothy. *Making Sense of God: An Invitation to the Sceptical.* Hodder & Stoughton Ltd, 2018.

Lennox, John C. *Gunning for God: Why the New Atheists Are Missing the Target.* Lion, 2011.

Ley, David J. *Ethical Porn for Dicks: A Man's Guide to Responsible Viewing Pleasure.* ThreeL Media, 2016.

Levitin, Daniel J. *The Organized Mind: Thinking Straight in the Age of Information Overload.* Dutton an Imprint of Penguin Random House, 2017.

Long, Stephen. *Christian Ethics: A Very Short Introduction.* Oxford University Press, 2010.

MacAskill, William. *Doing Good Better: Effective Altruism and a Radical New Way to Make a Difference.* Faber & Faber, 2016.

Malik, Kenan. *The Quest for a Moral Compass: A Global History of Ethics.* Atlantic Books, 2015.

Marks, Jonathan M. *What It Means to Be 98% Chimpanzee: Apes, People, and Their Genes.* Univ. of California Press, 2005.

Martin, Robert M., and Andrew Bailey. *First Philosophy: Fundamental Problems and Readings in Philosophy.* Broadview Press, 2012.

McCarthy, Matt. *Superbugs: The Race to Stop an Epidemic.* Scribe Publications, 2019.

Metaxas, Eric. *Martin Luther: The Man Who Rediscovered God and Changed the World.* Penguin Books, 2018.

"Moral Tribes: Emotion, Reason, and the Gap Between Us and Them by Joshua Greene – Review." Gray, John. *The Guardian*, Guardian News and Media, 17 Jan. 2014, www.theguardian.com/books/2014/jan/17/moral-tribes-joshua-greene-review.

Nicholls, William. *Christian Antisemitism: A History of Hate.* Rowman & Littlefield Pub., 2004.

Ord, Toby. *The Precipice: Existential Risk and the Future of Humanity.* Bloomsbury, 2020.

"Peter Singer: On Racism, Animal Rights and Human Rights." Yancy , George. *The New York Times*, 2015, opinionator.blogs.nytimes.com/2015/05/27/peter-singer-on-speciesism-and-racism/.

Perry, William James, and Tom Z. Collina. *The Button: The New Nuclear Arms Race and Presidential Power from Truman to Trump.* BenBella Books, Inc., 2020.

Pinker, Steven. *Enlightenment Now: The Case for Reason, Science, Humanism, and Progress.* Penguin Books, 2019.

Pinker, Steven. *The Better Angels of Our Nature: Why Violence Has Declined.* Viking, 2011.

Piper, John. "Think: The Life of the Mind and the Love of God." Crossway, 2010.

Reese, Jacy. *The End of Animal Farming: How Scientists, Entrepreneurs, and Activists Are Building an Animal-Free Food System.* Beacon Press, 2019.

Russell, Bertrand. *Why I am Not a Christian.* Simon & Schuster, inc. 1957.

Schaeffer, Francis August. *Pollution and the Death of Man: The Christian View of Ecology.* Tyndale House Publishers, 1981.

Shanor, Karen, and Jagmeet S. Kanwal. *Bats Sing Mice Giggle: Revealing the Secret Lives of Animals.* Icon, 2010.

Shermer, Michael. *The Moral Arc: How Science and Reason Lead Humanity toward Truth, Justice, and Freedom.* Henry Holt and Co., 2015.

Singer, Peter. *Ethics in the Real World: 82 Brief Essays on Things That Matter.* Princeton University Press, 2016.

Singer, Peter. *The Most Good You Can Do: How Effective Altruism Is Changing Ideas about Living Ethically.* The Text Publishing Company, 2016.

Smith, Wesley J. *A Rat Is a Pig Is a Dog Is a Boy: The Human Cost of the Animal Rights Movement.* Encounter Books, 2012.

Stanovich, Keith E. *The Robot's Rebellion: Finding Meaning in the Age of Darwin.* University of Chicago Press, 2004.

Stewart, Robert M. *Readings in Social and Political Philosophy.* Oxford University Press, 1996.

"The Case against Human Rights | Eric Posner." Posner, Eric. *The Guardian,* Guardian News and Media, 4 Dec. 2014, www.theguardian.com/news/2014/dec/04/-sp-case-against-human-rights.

"The Meaning of Marriage | Timothy Keller | Talks at Google." *YouTube,* Talks at Google, 2011, www.youtube.com/watch?v=C9THu0PZwwk.

"The Way the World Thinks - Albert Mohler." *YouTube,* Truth Endures, 2010, www.youtube.com/watch?v=YdN4-lX48U4.

"Tuesday, August 11, 2020." Mohler, Albert. *Albertmohler.com,* 2020, albert-mohler.com/2020/08/11/briefing-8-11-20?fbclid=IwAR3eOQIbYlcUK8 DAYdNsX6tYjY4BeTI89i8zMG3EGrs4q2QJ94ZdXr0bmF4.

United Nations High Commissioner for Refugees. "Figures at a Glance." *UNHCR,* 2019, www.unhcr.org/figures-at-a-glance.html.

Wallace-Wells, David. *The Uninhabitable Earth: Life after Warming.* Tim Duggan Books, 2019.

Watson, Peter. *The Age of Atheists: How We Have Sought to Live since the Death of God.* Simon & Schuster, 2014.

"We Have to Wake up: Factory Farms Are Breeding Grounds for Pandemics | Jonathan Safran Foer and Aaron S Gross." Foer, Jonathan Safran, and Aaron S Gross. *The Guardian,* Guardian News and Media, 20 Apr. 2020, www.theguardian.com/commentisfree/2020/apr/20/factory-farms-pandemic-risk-covid-animal-human-health.

"Why Are You so Afraid of Subjective Moral Reasoning?" *YouTube*, Ravi Zacharias International Ministries, 2014, www.youtube.com/watch?v=0218GkAGbnU.

"Why Knowledge and Logic Are Political Dirty Words." Kakutani, Michiko. *The New York Times*, 11 Mar. 2008, www.nytimes.com/2008/03/11/books/11kaku.html.

Wright, Robert. *The Evolution of God.* Abacus, 2013.

"Yuval Noah Harari & Natalie Portman." *YouTube*, How to Academy, 2018, https://www.youtube.com/watch?v=87XFTJXH9sc.

Zacharias, K., Ravi, and Durant, Danielle. *Beyond Opinion: Living the Faith That We Defend.* Thomas Nelson, 2010.

Zmirak, John. "Systemic Racism and Other Conspiracy Theories." *The Stream*, 11 June 2020, stream.org/systemic-racism-and-other-conspiracy-theories/.

Zuckerman, Phil. *Living the Secular Life: New Answers to Old Questions.* Penguin Press, 2014.

About The Author

Jakub Ferencik

Jakub Ferencik is a blogger, author, and musician. His blog on Medium.com has received more than 1 million visits. He is originally from Slovakia but primarily resides in Canada. He has studied Philosophy and Political Science at the University of British Columbia.